CHAMPIONS!

THE GREATEST SPORTS LEGENDS OF ALL TIME

CHAMPIONS!
THE GREATEST SPORTS LEGENDS OF ALL TIME

ANGUS G. GARBER III

MALLARD
PRESS

MALLARD PRESS
An imprint of BDD Promotional Book Company, Inc.
666 Fifth Avenue
New York, New York 10103

A FRIEDMAN GROUP BOOK
Published by MALLARD PRESS
An imprint of BDD Promotional Book Company, Inc.
666 Fifth Avenue
New York, New York 10103

ISBN 0-792-45244-5

CHAMPIONS!: The Greatest Sports Legends of All Time
was prepared and produced by
Michael Friedman Publishing Group, Inc.
15 West 26th Street
New York, New York 10010

Editor: Sharon Kalman
Art Director: Jeff Batzli
Designer: Kevin Ullrich
Photography Editor: Christopher Bain
Photo Researcher: Daniella Jo Nilva
Production: Karen L. Greenberg
Typeset by: Mar + X Myles Graphics Inc.
Color separations by United South Sea
Graphic Art Co., Ltd.
Printed and Bound in Hong Kong by South China Printing Co. (1988) Ltd.

Dedication

For Emily Anne Garber

Acknowledgments

Thanks to: Don Smith of the Pro Football Hall of Fame; the Basketball Hall of Fame's Wayne Patterson; Jeffery Denomme of the Hockey Hall of Fame; the International Tennis Hall of Fame's Jan Armstrong; Peter May, Bob Sudyk, and Claire Smith of the *Hartford Courant*; reference librarian extraordinaire Suzanne M. Garber; the insight of the legendary Grantland Rice; Bruce Lubin and Sharon Kalman of the Michael Friedman Publishing Group; the National Broadcasting Corporation; the *New York Post*'s Henry Gola; publisher Steven Weitzen.

Table of Contents

Introduction

MARK SPITZ GREW UP IN MODESTO, CALIFORNIA, a child of privilege. His father, a driven and successful man, moved the entire family to insure that Mark had the finest swimming facilities available to him in his quest for excellence. In 1960, twelve years before Spitz won seven gold medals at the Summer Olympic Games in Munich, West Germany, Florence Griffith-Joyner was born in Los Angeles, some 300 miles down the California coast, yet worlds away from the idyllic setting Spitz enjoyed as a youngster. Griffith-Joyner, one of eleven children, grew up in the grimy projects where moving was not an option and swimming pools weren't exactly a part of the childhood experience. She ran on hard asphalt and by the time she reached the Summer Olympic Games in Seoul, South Korea, in 1988, she was a world-class sprinter. Like Spitz, Griffith-Joyner brought home the gold, three all told.

There are no prerequisites for the champions you will find chronicled here. They are all sizes and shapes: from a puckish 4-foot-11, 84-pound Soviet gymnast named Olga Korbut, to Kareem Abdul-Jabbar, the 7-foot-2, 267-pound basketball center for the Los Angeles Lakers. Background is no guarantee of success or failure. Tennis star Martina Navratilova, who at age eleven watched in terror as tanks rolled into Prague, Czechoslovakia, later defected to America and developed into the best athlete in her profession. Bobby Jones grew up on a golf course in Atlanta, mastered it at the age of twelve, won the Georgia Amateur title at fourteen, and the United States Open at twenty-one. Temperament also seems to have no consistent bearing on athletic success. Hammerin' Hank Aaron was almost terminally beatific at the plate, while Ty Cobb was a tyrant who sharpened his spikes and liked to show them on the basepaths.

There are some common denominators, of course. Determination is the one thing all these legendary athletes share, often from a very early age. The ability and inclination to sacrifice time for training surfaces again and again. There is a passion to succeed here that, at times, transcends all else. The innate drive that powers each right-hand punch by heavyweight champion Mike Tyson is the same impulse behind Steffi Graf's vicious forehand. In essence, the will to win is what makes these champions excel in their various arenas. For what it's worth, it doesn't hurt to have a domineering parent, or a different perspective on life.

Coaches are another important factor. Several of the finest in their respective sports are represented here, including Vince Lombardi of the Green Bay Packers and Red Auerbach of the Boston Celtics, two men with radically different approaches to athletics. Only their spectacular results are similar.

Here they are, from the meat-and-potatoes sports of baseball and football, to soccer, boxing, and track and field, in all their glory.

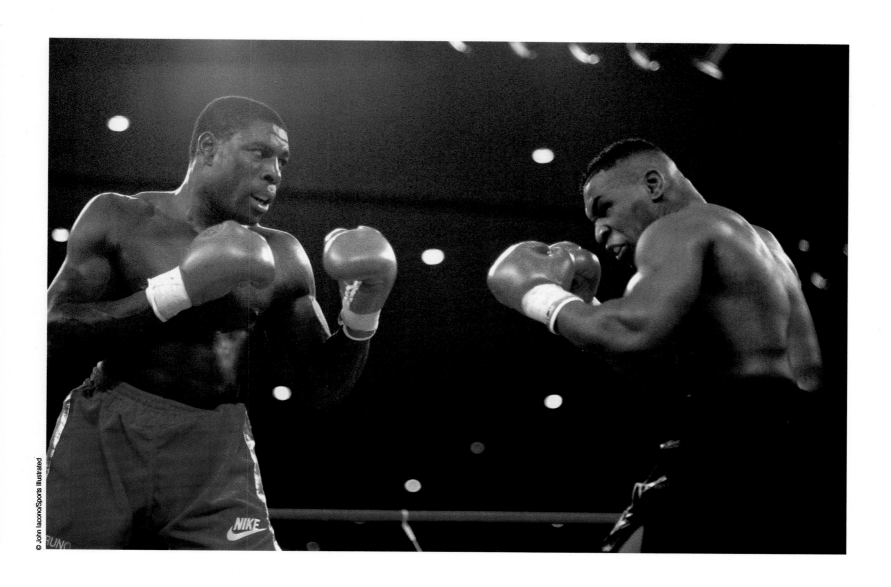

9

Hank Aaron

The gentle power of Hank Aaron could be seen in his supple wrists and unwavering concentration at the plate.

© Manny Rubio

 HENRY LOUIS AARON NEVER TRULY excited the baseball critics the way Willie Mays or Babe Ruth did; flamboyance was not his strong suit. Rather, Aaron was brilliantly consistent. On April 8, 1974, his smooth, economical swing brought him to the threshold of baseball's most hallowed mark.

A crowd of 53,775 was stuffed into Atlanta Stadium that night, each fan hoping that the Braves' left fielder would unleash those sweet wrists and send another ball over the fence. With a huge national television audience watching, Al Downing of the Los Angeles Dodgers walked Aaron on five pitches the first time he batted. Downing threw another ball in the fourth inn-

ing, before Aaron finally connected at 9:07 p.m. It was a fastball, a little too fast, and Aaron hit it over the wall in left field into the glove of teammate Tom House, who was patrolling the Braves' bullpen. At the age of forty, Aaron had hit the 715th home run of his career, breaking the record set by Babe Ruth thirty-nine years earlier. The final number, 755, is the new standard in baseball. Not quite as well known are the other all-time records that Aaron produced over his twenty-four-year career: 2,297 runs batted in (RBI's); 6,856 total bases; and 1,477 extra-base hits.

The raw numbers are difficult to digest. Throw out the first and last three years of his career and Aaron averaged thirty-six home runs a year for his middle

© Manny Rubio

Below: As soon as the ball came off the bat, Aaron, Dodgers catcher Joe Ferguson, and umpire David Davidson knew home run Number 715 had been hit. Right: Most baseball fans don't know it, but Aaron played first, second, and third base, as well as a commanding role in the outfield.

eighteen seasons. He led the National League in homers and runs batted in four different times, and in runs scored on three occasions. True, he was a slugger (he led the league in slugging percentage four times), but Aaron also had a marvelous eye at the plate. His career batting average was a sturdy .305, and early in his career, before the pursuit of home runs brought a subtle uppercut to his swing, Aaron twice led the league in hitting, with averages of .328 and .355. Remarkably, considering his production numbers, this slugger rarely struck out. Over his career he averaged only sixty strikeouts for every 537 at-bats. And in twenty-four years, Aaron never missed an All-Star game.

Though Jackie Robinson had broken the color barrier in baseball four years earlier with the Brooklyn Dodgers, life for a black baseball player in America wasn't all sweetness in 1951. Aaron was born on February 5, 1934 in Mobile, Alabama, and his gifts for the game were evident at an early age. The elegant 6-foot, 185-pounder was a boy playing against men. He left home at the precocious age of seventeen with a few dollars in his tattered pocket, two sandwiches, and some loose clothes. Aaron sought his fortune with the Indianapolis Clowns, a barnstorming team that placed a high value on entertainment. It wasn't particularly dignified, but it was a living. Fortunately, Aaron caught on with Eau Claire (Wisconsin) of the Northern League in 1952. He was a shortstop with large, soft hands. His average that year was .336, but he hit only nine home runs. A year later in Jacksonville, Mississippi, Aaron hit twenty-two homers and was given a chance to make the Milwaukee Braves big club in 1954.

By now, Aaron's hitting ability had been discovered and he was moved to the outfield. He played in 116 games as a rookie and batted a respectable .280. Though his thirteen home runs were hardly noteworthy, Aaron demonstrated a capacity for extra base hits, leading the National League in doubles his second and third seasons. In 1957, Aaron found the groove that would lift him into baseball's select group of superstars, which included Willie Mays and Mickey Mantle. He hit forty-four home runs that season, along with 132 RBI's, 118 runs scored, a batting average of .322, and a slugging percentage of .600. That was the season Aaron won the Most Valuable Player Award and hit three home runs as the Braves beat the New York Yankees in a stirring seven-game World Series. Six years later, Aaron's consistency was underlined with a similar season that resulted in another forty-four homers, 130 RBI's, 121 runs scored, and a .319 batting average.

In 1971, at the age of thirty-seven, Aaron posted his best single-season homer mark, with forty-seven. Typical of his career he never posted the spectacular single-season numbers of Ruth or Roger Maris. No, Aaron was methodical in his run toward history. In 1973, at thirty-nine, he hit an even forty-homers to set the stage for his record-breaking game a season later. Aaron finished out the last two years of his career with the Milwaukee Brewers, where he started, and pushed the game's most recognizable number to 755.

Kareem Abdul-Jabbar

Abdul-Jabbar's agility was startling for a man taller than 7-foot-3. His chief contribution was bringing athletic talent to the center's position.

 NO ONE EVER DID IT BETTER, FOR longer, on a basketball court than Kareem Abdul-Jabbar. The National Basketball Association record book is virtually his; Abdul-Jabbar holds the highest standards in seasons played (twenty), games played (more than 1,500), minutes played (56,000), points (38,000), field goals (15,000), and blocked shots (3,000). Yet his dominance is best seen in his glory decade, the 1970s. Abdul-Jabbar averaged 23.8 points and 14.4 rebounds per game in that time, and took home an incredible six Most Valuable Player Awards to go with nine All-Star appearances.

Boston Celtics center Robert Parish remembers one night, November 19, 1976, when Abdul-Jabbar scored twenty-eight points and pulled down twenty rebounds in an easy Los Angeles Lakers victory over the Golden State Warriors. "It was an experience," Parish says of his first encounter with the great center. "I played two, three, maybe four minutes because he already had given George Johnson and Clifford Ray all they wanted. He was unusually warm that night. Everything went in. I remember thinking, 'Does he ever miss?' It was unbelievable."

Born in New York City on April 16, 1947 with the name Ferdinand Lewis Alcindor, it was clear that he was marked for greatness from the beginning. Alcindor led Power Memorial Academy to a 95-6 record, including seventy-one straight victories. The University of California at Los Angeles won the heavy recruiting

© R. Mackson/FPG International

Above: He could dribble and pass, but what he did best was intimidate at both ends of the floor. Right: On defense, he changed the way opponents approached his team; on offense he was the closest thing to unstoppable the NBA has ever seen.

battle for his services, and the 7-foot-2, 235-pound center responded with 33 points per game as a freshman. UCLA won the next three National Collegiate Athletic Association championships with Alcindor taking the tournament's Most Valuable Player honors all three times. The success never seemed to come easily, though; Alcindor was almost too sensitive and thoughtful for the bruising game of basketball. "I'm basically serious, but I laugh at a lot of things," he said once. "I'm not schizophrenic, it's just that people relate to me either as a basketball player or a 7-foot object, not as a person. That's what I have to deal with. I was always taller than other kids, but I was younger, too. You kind of withdraw in that situation. The things you don't know about, you let go by. After awhile, it became my natural demeanor."

Following his Islamic religion, he changed his name to Kareem Abdul-Jabbar and, over the years developed a virtually unblockable shot to go with his smooth moves around the basket. The shot is called the Skyhook, and the majority of Abdul-Jabbar's points have come from this long-armed hook shot that is actually released above the basket. When he joined the Milwaukee Bucks in 1969, the torch was passed, in effect, from centers Bill Russell and Wilt Chamberlain. Russell had retired from the Celtics during the off-season and Chamberlain was well past his prime. Abdul-Jabbar's rookie season was fairly modest by his later standards, but he averaged nearly 29 points and 14 rebounds a game. As he grew into his body (he would eventually stand 7-feet-3⅜ inches and weigh close to 270 pounds), Abdul-Jabbar came to dominate the NBA. With the addition of aging wizard

Oscar Robertson, the Bucks won sixty-six games and the league title in 1971.

Abdul-Jabbar moved to the Lakers in 1975, and six years later the pieces were in place for a rare team, indeed. With Jabbar at the team's center and guard Magic Johnson running the show, Los Angeles won world titles in 1980, 1982, 1985, 1987, and 1988. As players like Johnson and James Worthy took on increasing responsibilities, Abdul-Jabbar could afford to become more of a team player. With time, many important NBA records fell. In 1980, he was named to the league's Thirty-fifth Anniversary All-Time Team, and on April 5, 1984, a Skyhook against the Utah Jazz broke Wilt Chamberlain's career scoring record.

Though no player in league history ever lasted past seventeen seasons, Abdul-Jabbar found the will to survive, even thrive, into his twentieth season, a career that extended into three decades. The lure of championship rings (he has six) and a three-million-dollar salary kept him interested. Abdul-Jabbar's consistency over the years was nothing short of phenomenal. He averaged 20 points per game for fifteen straight seasons and scored in double figures in 466 consecutive games in the 1980s. As impressive as his career has been, Abdul-Jabbar will be mostly remembered for his dominance in the 1970s. Tree Rollins of the Atlanta Hawks likes to talk about his first meeting with Abdul-Jabbar, on December 12, 1977. "It was an exciting moment for me," he said. "I was hyped up and my big ambition was to block one of those Skyhooks. I got my chance and I did. It was the worst thing that I ever did. He came back down and made seven in a row. Then, for good measure, he threw one in left-handed. I guess it wasn't such a good idea to block it, but it was thrilling, for about two minutes. Then it was a nightmare."

Muhammad Ali

FROM THE BEGINNING, IT WAS clear Cassius Marcellus Clay, Jr., was going to be something special. "When a baby, he would never sit down," his mother Odessa wrote in her journal. "When I would take him for a stroll in his stroller, he would always stand up and try to see everything. He tried to walk at a very early age. He tried so hard, he learned to walk at ten months old. He walked on his toes and, by doing this, has well-developed arches, and that is why he is so fast on his feet." His father added, "Yeah, and he loved to talk." One day, that blinding speed of foot and mouth would be his trademark.

Ali was born on January 17, 1942 in Louisville, Kentucky and stumbled into boxing at twelve. Someone had stolen his bicycle, and the scrawny adolescent came to Joseph Martin, the director of boxing for the

Louisville Recreation Department, looking for revenge of a sort. "He wanted to whip someone," said Martin, a Louisville policeman, "but he had never boxed before." Young Clay trained faithfully until he was first thrown into the ring, all eighty-nine pounds of him, against a boy named Ronny O'Keefe at the Columbia Gym. They fought like cats that Saturday night, and Clay had discovered his calling. He would miss a year between the ages of fifteen and sixteen when doctors discovered a heart murmur, but by the time he reached Rome's Palazzo dello Sporto in 1960, Clay had fought more than one hundred amateur fights and won forty-three straight.

Though most athletes at the Summer Olympic Games were merely happy to be there, this Louisville slugger entertained reporters with his breezy candor. "Why try to tell myself, 'Maybe I'll win,'" Clay said, "when I really think I will?" Even as he moved into the ring for the light-heavyweight final against Ziggy Pietrzykowski of Poland, a left-handed bronze medalist from the 1956 Games with 231 previous bouts, Clay appeared unaware of the stakes involved as he clowned and preened. In many ways, his behavior belied his intense preparation for the event of his life; Clay's roommates in the Olympic Village complained that he shadowboxed into the early hours of the morning. It took two rounds for the American to figure Pietrzykowski out, but the flash of Clay's fists in the third round left the Pole with a mask of blood as the final bell rang. Clay, toasted as the world's greatest amateur boxer, immediately decided to turn professional.

"He was pretty much unspoiled," remembers Dr. Ferdie Pacheco, Ali's physician. "It was as if they'd taken a can and opened it up and out came this eighteen-year-old with his childish ideas of fame and fortune." They all came true, for Cassius Clay was a rare talent, both in and out of the ring. He floated like a butterfly, stung like a bee, as he liked to say, and eventually became sport's most charismatic athlete in the 1960s and 1970s. His championship debut on February 25, 1964, left most people in boxing speechless. Clay, who fought his first and last title fight under that name before changing it to the Muhammad Ali of Muslim custom, was an eight-to-one underdog against Sonny Liston. Despite a pair of one-round knockouts of former champion Floyd Patterson, Liston looked sluggish against the silky-smooth fighter from Louisville. Liston failed to answer the bell for the sixth round and the world had a new heavyweight champion.

Ali's first-round knockout of Liston fifteen months later in Lewiston, Maine underlined what was already obvious: Here was a champion for the ages. Deploying a frightening combination of speed and power, Ali defended his title nine times. He could slug inside, or dance around the ring's periphery, coyly ducking out

© AP/Wide World Photos, Inc.

© Ken Kaminsky/FPG International

of the way of punches as they whistled by his head. Ali's successful defense against Zora Folley on March 22, 1967 was his last fight for four years, since he was stripped of his title for failing to enlist in the United States Army for religious reasons. While Ali watched from the sidelines, Joe Frazier and Jimmy Ellis won the two heavyweight championships (The WBC and the WBA, respectively). On March 8, 1971, Ali returned to the ring to fight Frazier in the first of three celebrated bouts. He lost on points over fifteen rounds, but undoubtedly was back. Two years later, George Foreman knocked Frazier senseless in Kingston, Jamaica to win the title.

Becoming only the second man in history to regain the heavyweight championship, Ali knocked out Foreman in the eighth round of their October 30, 1974 fight in Kinshasa, Zaire. Battling the oppressive heat, Ali rested on the ropes and, at well chosen times, unleashed a barrage of furious punches to win the heavyweight championship. Ali reigned for more than three years and beat Frazier, among others, before running into the unorthodox Leon Spinks. On February 18, 1978, Ali lost a fifteen-round decision to Spinks. This set up Ali's attempt to win a record three heavyweight titles. Seven months later, Ali took the title back from Spinks with a complete display of ringsmanship. When he lost the title a final time to Larry Holmes in 1980, Ali's skills had diminished greatly. Still, he finished his career with fifty-six victories, five defeats, and thirty-seven knockouts. Moreover, he had influenced a generation of fighters, who mimicked his gregarious pre-fight monologues and flashy punch combinations, and mesmerized the American public with both his wit and his fists.

More than anything, Ali brought showbiz charisma to the ring. His razor-sharp reflexes allowed him to elude even the quickest punchers; his iron will helped him rise above the toughest punches.

Mario Andretti

THE IDEA FIRST TOOK HOLD IN Lucca, Italy, where thirteen-year-old Mario Andretti and his twin brother, Aldo, parked cars for a local garage. That led to motorcycles and, in a short time, the Junior Grand Prix circuit, a government-subsidized venture to improve post-war morale. When Alberto Ascari and his Lancia won a thrilling wheel-to-wheel duel with Juan Manuel Fangio in the 1954 Grand Prix of Monza, young Mario knew his destiny lay in auto racing.

A year later, the large Andretti family moved to Nazareth, Pennsylvania, a severe blow to the twins' racing aspirations. Eventually, the two scraped together a 1948 Hudson Hornet, built from pieces they scavenged all over town, taking care to keep the news from their parents. The final cost was $807 and, after a coin flip, Aldo won the right to race it April 25, 1959, at Nazareth Speedway. He won easily, going away collecting ninety dollars for his trouble. The following week, Mario duplicated the feat. A brutal accident later that season at Hatfield left Mario as the sole driver.

Andretti moved up the racing ladder in fairly conventional style. During 1960 and 1961, Andretti started forty-six stock car races and won twenty-one. Then he graduated to sprint cars and suffered through the only prolonged slump of his career. The open cockpits of the United Racing Club series were a distraction; twenty starts yielded a season's best of eighth in the main event—and a new talent for picking the dirt out of his teeth. The experts concluded that Andretti, all of 130 pounds, was too small to succeed. Nonetheless, he managed to convince his father-in-law, Earl Hoch, to purchase a three-quarter midget car in return for half of the gross. On January 6, 1962, Andretti placed tenth in the thirty-five-lap feature at Teaneck, New Jersey, moving *National Speed Sports News* to observe, "This was Mario Andretti's first indoor ride. He is a graduate of the URC sprint ranks and he impressed." Three days after his twenty-second birthday, Andretti won his first midget feature at Teaneck. Seven years later, he would win the Indianapolis 500.

Andretti started thirty-three indoor races and placed in the top ten twenty-four times before stepping up to a higher class of midget cars. By late 1963, Andretti had reached the threshold. His first United States Auto Club sprint race came at the Allentown Fair in Pennsylvania, with people like A.J. Foyt and Jim

Even at the wheel of a million-dollar machine, Mario Andretti pushes it like the 1948 Hudson Hornet he pieced together and first raced in 1959. That kind of drive is what makes Andretti one of the very best at his particular craft.

Andretti still competes for the top racing prizes, though his son, Michael, pushes him at every turn.

McElreath in the field. Andretti placed fourteenth in that event, but soon after he was to win two national championships. His first title, a 100-mile race at Trenton, New Jersey, led to a publicized testing session for Firestone. In May 1964, Andretti left his full-time job of assembling golf carts for Motovator, Inc. and headed for the midwest. His success there led to an opportunity with car-owner Clint Brawner. Andretti became one of the perennial leaders and, in 1965, made his first start at the Indianapolis 500. Andretti placed third, behind Jimmy Clark and Parnelli Jones, and took home $42,551 and Rookie-of-the-Year honors.

Andretti won the Daytona 500 in 1967 and, finally, took the Indy 500 two years later. In characteristic, hard-charging fashion, Andretti drove Andy Granatelli's STP Oil Treatment Special #2 to victory at an average speed of 156.8 miles an hour, a race record.

Since then, Andretti has achieved virtually everything an auto racer can, and more. These days, his son Michael races against him on the Indianapolis car circuit and Mario wouldn't have it any other way. Even today, he still races with a seat-of-the-pants enthusiasm that takes you back to those scrambling sprint car events of the early 1960s.

Though he is known today as the architect of so many successful Boston Celtics teams, the franchise president, Arnold "Red" Auerbach, was also a terrific coach.

Red Auerbach

EVERYBODY LOVES A WINNER, THOUGH Arnold Red Auerbach's unprecedented coaching success in the National Basket-ball Association quite naturally rubbed some of his peers the wrong way. After all, it is no fun getting smoke from a victory cigar blown in your face night after night, year after year. Yet when he walked away from coaching while still in his prime, at the age of forty-eight, Auerbach's genius couldn't be denied. His twenty-year mark of 1,037 victories stands as an NBA record and was balanced by only 548 losses, a staggering winning percentage of better than sixty-five. Moreover, Auerbach's Boston Celtics dominated basketball as no professional team ever has, in any sport. The Celtics, led by players such as Bill Russell,

John Havlicek, K.C. and Sam Jones, Bob Cousy, Tom Heinsohn, and Frank Ramsey, delivered nine championships in ten seasons for Auerbach. In many ways, Auerbach remains the living definition of Celtic pride, an intangible quality that has become a way of life in Boston and a goal for coaches in other disciplines.

When he arrived in the NBA in 1946, Auerbach's resumé did not suggest instant success. He was born in Brooklyn, New York on September 20, 1917, and spent a good deal of time trying to learn the craft of basketball. At five-foot-ten, 170 pounds, Auerbach was a guard, after a fashion. He played at Eastern District High School, then moved on to Seth Low Junior College in New York City. Auerbach's statistics there aren't available, which is probably just as well; in three subsequent seasons at George Washington University, in Washington, D.C., Auerbach averaged just six points per game. After World War II, he emerged as the coach of the Washington Capitols in the fledgling NBA. The Caps posted a league-best 49-11 record and, following stops at Tri-Cities (a former NBA team) and Duke University, Auerbach took the reigns in Boston, at the age of thirty-four.

Coaching ability has always been a difficult thing to quantify; at its very essence, it is a transference of confidence, of values, and of ideals. So, while Auerbach did not bring a can't-miss jump shot to the Celtics, he carried with him a sensitivity and attention to detail that served him well over the years. Like many of baseball's great managers, Auerbach learned the subtleties of his sport, because his talent hadn't been enough. "In the early 1940s, when I was in the Navy, I met Phil Rizzuto and we talked about the way Joe McCarthy managed those great Yankee clubs," Auerbach said. "Phil told me how Joe would take rookies from the farms and teach them little things like tipping properly in restaurants and acting properly in hotel lobbies. Joe was vitally concerned with the image of the Yankees. He believed the way you acted off the field had a great deal to do with the way you performed on it. I decided that any club I ever coached would be imbued with this philosophy: Dress like a champion, act like a champion, and you'll play like a champion. Celtic pride was no myth, no fairy tale, but pride was only a part of what made us what we were. For a player to feel good about his team and teammates, he must also feel good about his role in the team's success."

Still, it takes a few great players to make a great coach, and Auerbach was blessed with many of the greatest names in basketball. His great gift, however, came in convincing his players that the team's pursuit of victory was more important than meeting personal goals. This explains why the Celtics have produced sixteen championship banners over the years, yet not one Boston player has ever led the league in scoring. In a game that often digresses into individual play, the Celtics actually pass the ball.

Auerbach took a 22-46 team to a record of 39-30 in the 1950 season Their record at Boston Garden was a phenomenal 26-6, a sign that Auerbach's beliefs were taking hold.

In 1956, Auerbach first demonstrated his unmatched eye for talent when he traded established stars Ed Macauley and Cliff Hagan for the rights to University of San Francisco center Bill Russell. Aided by Cousy and Bill Sharman, the rookie gave Auerbach his first NBA Championship. There would be eight more over the next nine seasons before Auerbach would retire as a coach in 1966 to become the Celtics' president and general manager. In some ways, Auerbach was even more effective in this role; he drafted Indiana State University forward Larry Bird as a junior-eligible, persuaded guard Danny Ainge to quit baseball for basketball, and made deals for Dennis Johnson, Kevin McHale, and Robert Parish.

In 1980, when the Celtics won yet another championship, Auerbach was named the NBA's Executive of the Year. That same season, the Professional Basketball Writers' Association voted him the Greatest Coach in NBA History.

Auerbach's career winning percentage of .662 stands as the NBA's best of all time. Here, he calls an offensive play during a timeout.

Sammy Baugh

Sammy Baugh changed the way quarterbacks passed in the NFL; that is his greatest legacy.

THE GREAT MAJORITY OF PROFESsional athletes merely pass through a sport, happy to contribute and earn a living. Sammy Baugh was one of those rare men whose excellence changed forever the way his discipline was played; when he retired from football after the 1952 season, "just passing through" had taken on a completely different meaning.

Baugh, a lean 6-foot-2, 180 pounds, was perceived as something of a radical when he broke in with the Washington Redskins in 1937. From its beginning, professional football had been built on the running game; now, a two-time All-America from Texas Christian University was trying to change all that. The Redskins, nee Boston Braves, had arrived in the nation's capital after the 1936 season. Owner George Marshall was looking for something to help sell his team. He chose Baugh in the first round of the college draft, signed him to a handsome salary of $5,000, and instructed coach Ray Flaherty to showcase the rookie. Flaherty, told Baugh, "You're going to have to learn to run. You can't get by up here by just passing like crazy."

Oh, but he could. Baugh had already succeeded in his debut against professionals, throwing a touchdown pass to Gaynell Tinsley for the only score against the world champion Green Bay Packers in the College All-Star Game. Baugh's rookie season, 1937, cast aside any doubts about the new-wave passing game. Former University of Alabama wide receiver Don Hutson had already begun the revolution two seasons earlier in Green Bay, and now Baugh began slicing up secondaries with ease. He completed eleven of sixteen passes in his first regular-season game, a 13-3 victory over the Giants. That year the Redskins rolled all the way to the NFL championship game. Baugh threw three monstrous touchdown passes and totaled 335 yards in the air. His thirty-five-yard scoring toss to Ed Justice gave the Redskins a 28-21 victory over the Chicago Bears at Wrigley Field. So much for running.

Baugh lined up as a single-wing tailback for eight years with the Redskins and led the league three times in passing before new coach Dudley DeGroot made the long-anticipated switch, in 1944, to the T-formation that Baugh's success had helped popularize. As a quarterback, Baugh was even more dangerous; he led the league three more times, pushing his total to six passing titles—two more than any other quarterback in NFL history. San Francisco 49'ers gifted quarterback Joe Montana, for instance, has won that honor only once.

In 1945, he completed 128 of 182 passes for a completion percentage of 70.33, a record that held until Cincinnati's Ken Anderson managed 70.55 in 1982. Baugh's quarterback rating of 109.9 that season was the second-best mark in history. When Baugh retired in 1952, he had thrown for 21,886 yards and 186 touchdowns. He led the league in completion percentage for seven seasons, and placed first in yards passing four other times.

There was more to Baugh than a powerful passing arm. He was also the greatest punter in NFL history and a terrific defensive back. In 1943, Baugh led the league in passing, punting, and interceptions. He produced eleven interceptions and finished his career with a total of twenty-eight. There were four punting titles in Baugh's career, including a phenomenal 51.4 yards per kick in 1940, a record that may never be broken. Baugh's career average of 45.1 is also an NFL standard.

Born on March 17, 1914 in Temple, Texas, Baugh grew up throwing a football at a spare tire in his backyard. His college coach, Dutch Meyer, used him as a single-wing tailback who could run, throw, quick-kick, or pitch the ball to a teammate trailing the play. Baugh's size and seeming frailty was questioned once he joined the NFL. Early in his career, an opposing tackle knocked him down and hit him with a fist for good measure. When it happened again on the next play, with a knee thrown in, Baugh asked his linemen to let the defender through cleanly. Sure enough, in he came, and as he bore down on Baugh, the quarterback cocked his arm cooly and drilled him, right between the eyes, knocking him unconscious and out of the game. Sammy Baugh always got his man.

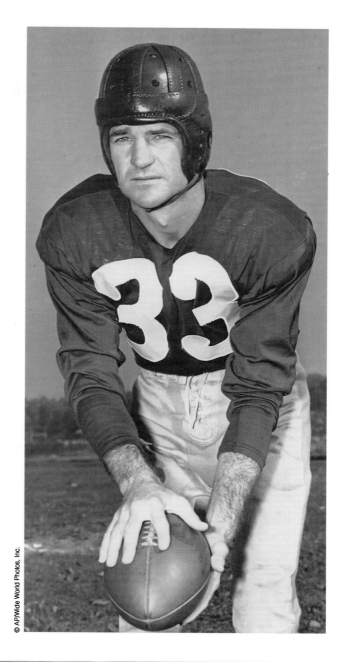

Even when his offensive line protection broke down, as in this October 10, 1942 game against the Chicago Bears (below), Baugh's eyes never left his intended target.

© AP/Wide World Photos, Inc.

© AP/Wide World Photos, Inc.

Bob Beamon

After setting a world record of 49 feet, 5 inches in the triple jump at the Penn Relays, Bob Beamon put his best feet forward.

 THERE ARE RARE TIMES WHEN MAN takes such a huge stride that the passage of time is necessary to put the accomplishment in perspective. Such was the case with the lunar landing in 1969. A year earlier, a high jumper named Bob Beamon produced a similar giant leap for mankind in Mexico City, Mexico.

They talked about the thin air at the Summer Olympics in 1968 and indeed, some startling milestones were achieved. Lee Evans churned through the 400-meters in 43.86 seconds; the triple-jump record was set and re-set nine times before Viktor Saneev of the Soviet Union pushed the standard past fifty-seven feet. There was no doubt that 27 percent less atmospheric pressure and 23 percent less air density at 7,300 feet above sea level had a hand in the unusual circumstances. Yet, that cannot explain what Beamon, a twenty-two-year-old American, did on October 18, 1968.

That Beamon, born August 29, 1936 in Jamaica, New York, had talent was indisputable; he was long and lean and could run 100 yards in a swift 9.5 seconds. Still, he was erratic and his best previous long jump was twenty-seven feet, four inches, less than an inch off the world record. Beamon lined up for his jump in the first round, trying to digest the advice of colleague Ralph Boston. Boston had won the long jump gold medal in the 1960 Games at Rome, Italy, and was friendly with Beamon, a competitor he regarded as gifted, if undisciplined. Before Mexico City, Beamon had used an approach completely devoid of forethought. When Boston suggested a preconceived stride pattern, Beamon took it under advisement.

Though Beamon sprinted down the runway close to top speed, he was under control. Hitting the board just short of a foul, Beamon soared through the air, swinging his slender arms and extending his long legs toward the sand. His mouth was wide open and his face bore an expression of amazement. That was nothing compared to the look Beamon offered after he finally came to earth, close to the edge of the pit. For a moment, officials worried that the prevailing wind was too strong and would wipe out the record-breaking jump. Measurements, however, proved that the wind speed was just under the maximum allowable two meters per second (4.47 miles an hour).

The enormity of the moment overwhelmed Beamon, who collapsed to the track when the distance appeared on the stadium monitor: 8.90. That was in meters; the translation was twenty-nine feet, two and one-half inches—fifty-five centimeters or twenty-one and one-half inches further than any man had jumped before. The crowd in the stadium rose in tribute as word spread. Beamon won the gold medal that day, but never came close to his record again. His best was twenty-six feet, eleven inches after he turned professional in 1973.

In 1988, time caught up with two of the three magnificent world records set twenty years earlier in the rarified air of Mexico City. American Butch Reynolds shattered Evans' mark in the 400 meters in Zurich, Switzerland six weeks before the Olympic Games in Seoul, South Korea. In those Games, the United States team of Danny Everett, Steve Lewis, Kevin Robinzine, and Reynolds equaled the 4 X 400-meter mark of 2:56.16 set by Vince Matthews, Ronald Freeman, George James, and Evans. And Carl Lewis won the long jump, with a leap of twenty-eight feet, seven and one-half inches—more than a half-foot short of Beamon's resounding jump. The record still stands today, a testament to a singular act of athletic skill and man's never-ending reach beyond his immediate grasp.

© Tony Duffy/AllSport

© AP/Wide World Photos, Inc.

Above: As he reached the apex of his epic jump, Beamon's mouth began to open in amazement over his own accomplishment. Left: As he fell to earth, the magnitude of his feat began to dawn on him. When the monitor flashed the distance of 8.90 meters, he collapsed.

He is not the tallest man to ever play professional basketball, nor the most mobile. Yet, Larry Bird is one of the best players in history because of his court savvy. Sometimes he even alters a shot to make it more challenging.

© Brian Drake/Sports Chrome, Inc.

Larry Bird

 SOMEHOW, THE VALUE OF LARRY Joe Bird, the consummate team player, wasn't discovered until he missed three months of the 1988-89 season with a foot injury. When Bird arrived in the National Basketball Association in 1979, the Boston Celtics were coming off a dreadful 29-53 season, the second-worst record in the NBA that year. In his first season, the Indiana State University rookie averaged twenty-one points and ten rebounds a game, and the Celtics finished with the league's best record, a 62-21 mark. From Bird's first month (November 1979), through November 1988, Boston posted a .500 or better record for a remarkable sixty-one consecutive months. With Bird sidelined following bone-spur surgery, Boston finally crashed, confirming suspicions among the basketball intelligencia that Bird was the straw that stirred the Celtics' drink. There are three NBA championship banners hanging in Boston Garden to prove it.

"That's why I play," he said. "I'm just greedy on them things. Winning the championship—I've never felt that way any other time, no matter how big some other game was. I remember the first time we won, against Houston [in 1981]. We were way ahead at the end, and so I came out with three minutes left, and my heart was pounding so on the bench, I thought it would jump out of my chest. You know what you feel? You just want everything to stop and stay like that forever."

Bird, one of basketball's most polished and complete athletes ever, plays with the same passion and eloquence he feels inside. At 6-foot-9, 220 pounds, he is perfectly proportioned and, according to Boston Celtics President Red Auerbach, perfect, period. "If I had to start a team," he said at a charity dinner in 1988, "the one guy in all of history I would take would be Larry Bird. This is the greatest ballplayer who ever played the game." This, from the man who coached Bill Russell, Bob Cousy, and John Havlicek and saw Kareem Abdul-Jabbar, Wilt Chamberlain, Magic Johnson, and Oscar Robertson play. Though Auerbach may be biased, he is not far from the truth.

Many athletes have been blessed with superior physical tools; Bird himself jokes that you can't slide a piece of paper under his sneakers when he jumps in the air. But rarely has a player understood the subtleties of his game the way Bird does. It is pure, innate reflex and it is a beautiful thing to behold. Such is his command of the court that Bird often tries a more difficult shot or pass out of sheer boredom. His teammates never cease to marvel at his creativity under pressure. Bird, however, did not come by these tools by accident. "You've got to understand," he said. "My whole life's been basketball. It was never a recreation for me. It was something I fell in love with."

Bird was born on December 7, 1956, in French Lick, Indiana, a midwest hotbed of basketball. Whatever French Lick (pop. 2,265) lacked in size and sophistication, it compensated with a competitive environment. Bird made the Springs Valley High School freshman team in 1970 and collected a twenty-dollar prize from his hard-driving father. Four years later, after a sensational high school career, Bird accepted a scholarship to Indiana University, a state-of-the-art program in college basketball. What might have been in Bloomington, we'll never know, for Bird was intimidated by the sprawling campus. He transferred to Indiana State and helped the Sycamores produce an 81-13 record in three seasons. Bird was virtually a one-man team, but he carried Indiana State to the 1979 National Collegiate Athletic Association Championship Game. Only Magic Johnson and a powerful Michigan State team were able to stop him.

Auerbach had seen all of this coming. He drafted Bird as a junior-eligible with the sixth overall pick in 1978. After that fabulous rookie season, Bird and the Celtics began to hit their stride. They beat the Houston Rockets for the NBA title in 1981, then repeated as champions in 1984 and 1986. Individually, Bird won three consecutive Most Valuable Player awards, in 1984, 1985, and 1986. Only Chamberlain and Russell ever managed that. Bird was also voted the playoff MVP in 1984 and 1986. Through nine seasons, Bird's game has remained well-rounded. He has averaged approximately twenty-four points, ten rebounds, six assists, and two steals per game. His concentration allowed him to lead the NBA in free-throw percentage in 1984, 1986, and 1987. That last season marked the first time a player ever shot 50 percent from the field and 90 percent from the free throw line. Most important, however, is Bird's ability to alter his game to particular circumstances. If the Celtics need rebounding, he sacrifices his scoring. If he is double-teamed, Bird becomes a point guard. "Whatever he wants to be," Auerbach said, "he is."

Bjorn Borg

ONE OF THE UNHAPPY DOWNSIDES of sports is the great athlete who lingers too long, whose skills fade before he leaves the arena. Bjorn Borg did not fall victim to this syndrome; the Swedish tennis artist left the game at the age of twenty-six, with five Wimbledon titles and six French Open championships on his shelf at home.

"If I had any regrets, I think I would have been back in tennis a long time ago," Borg said in 1988, a year after he was enshrined in the Tennis Hall of Fame in Newport, Rhode Island. "I felt that I was really locked in a room. I didn't really see the world. I didn't extend myself as a human being. I played tennis and, yes, I was very happy, but I wanted to improve myself as a human being, to learn more about life, to learn more about other things than how to play tennis. I knew sooner or later that [retirement] day would come anyway. I did not want to face that day when I was thirty-five or forty years old.

Bjorn Borg always looked the same: lean, impassive, focused. It was the secret to his success. Borg's intense concentration allowed him to hit thunderous shots with amazing consistency.

"I still like to compete. Even if I compete with my son, I still want to win. It was a matter of going out to practice four or five hours a day. In the end, I was asking myself, 'What are you doing?' "

Born on June 6, 1956 in Sodertalje, Sweden, Borg was playing tennis by the age of nine. His father, Rune, won a tennis racket in a local table-tennis tournament and soon young Borg was hitting a heavy, unorthodox forehand that seemed to be all wrist and topspin, and a strange, two-handed backhand. He was awkward, but he returned almost everything. Percy Rosburg, of the Swedish Tennis Federation, spotted Borg at the age of ten. "The federation wanted to change the two hands," he said. "But he could put the ball where he wanted it, that was the point. Oh, how he hit so hard. And, boy, he fought like hell." Borg never seemed to come off the court; one day in Malen, Sweden, Borg, thirteen at the time, played for nine hours, reaching the finals of five different age groups. By 1972, he had won the Junior Wimbledon crown and broke into the top ten rankings two years later. In 1973, Borg upset Arthur Ashe to reach the round of sixteen at the U.S. Open. In 1974, at seventeen, he won the French Open, thus becoming the youngest man ever to win one of tennis' grand-slam events. Borg had a hand in the 1975 Swedish Davis Cup victory, the same year he won his second straight French Open.

In 1976, at the age of twenty, Borg became the youngest Wimbledon men's champion in the modern era with a convincing win over Ilie Nastase. Borg's intense will to win and his topspin forehand were virtu-

His awesome concentration was not without cost, however. In 1982, at the age of twenty-six, he walked away from tennis forever.

ally unbeatable for a span of six years. Though his rackets were strung at eighty pounds per square inch, some twenty more than most professionals, Borg was still able to control the ball phenomenally well. Conditioning was another factor in the 5-foot-11, 165-pounder's success. Borg's resting heartbeat was once measured at thirty-eight beats per minute, half the norm. At the height of his game, Borg was making five million dollars a year in winnings and endorsements.

Borg's one great regret was his failure to win a U.S. Open title in ten years of trying. He reached the final four times only to lose, twice to Jimmy Connors. Some experts contend that Borg never recovered from the 1981 Open final, when John McEnroe won easily in four sets. Uncharacteristically, Borg skipped the awards ceremony and, perhaps coincidentally, embarked on an eighteen-month sabbatical. After battling with the Men's International Pro Tennis Council and Volvo Grand Prix during 1982 over the number of tournaments he would play, Borg passed on Wimbledon and the U.S. Open because he felt it was unfair to be forced to qualify. His last major victory came

in June 1981, when he won his sixth French Open. A month later he lost a classic Wimbledon final to McEnroe. That loss reversed the 1980 result, a five-set win for the Swede that many consider one of the best matches ever played.

Borg made his home in Monte Carlo, Monaco and spent an easy year there with his beautiful wife Mariana (from whom he is now divorced). It is no wonder he could not summon the will to climb back to the top. In November 1982, he surprised his wife one day with his decision to retire. "I have not got the right motivation," Borg said. "I cannot give one hundred percent, and if I cannot do that, it would not be fair to myself to go on. Tennis has to be fun if you are to get to the top, and I don't feel that way any more."

And today? "Mentally, I'm so far from tennis right now that if I should go out and play a match, I could concentrate maybe for one game. That's all. I still love the game. I'm always going to play tennis. I was playing tennis for eleven years as a professional. So far, those were the best years I've had, and I'm still only thirty-two."

Jim Brown

THOUGH THERE HAVE BEEN MEN who ran further and even more stylishly, no running back in National Football League history was better than Jim Brown. There is no argument from the football intelligencia. "When you look at it," said O.J. Anderson, himself the tenth leading rusher in league history, "nobody else is really close. What he did in that short time was amazing, really."

Walter Payton of the Chicago Bears is officially history's most prolific runner, with 16,726 yards gained, and in the coming years the Indianapolis Colts' Eric Dickerson is likely to surpass the 12,312-yard standard that Brown set from 1957-65. Yet Payton needed four more years and 1,479 more carries to produce that magnificent standard. In this day of multi-year contracts and advanced training techniques, the careers of professional athletes have been extended, leaving quality as the only fair measure of players from differ-

ent eras. Brown finished his career with the Cleveland Browns with the highest average per carry in history, 5.22, a record that endures today. Payton, by comparison, averaged only 4.36 yards per carry.

Consider his run of consistent excellence: In those nine seasons, Brown was voted by his peers to the Pro Bowl nine times, largely based on his league-leading rushing totals in eight of those seasons. That's right, Brown led the NFL in rushing for eight seasons, including five in a row, from 1957-61. Next in the league's record book are Steve Van Buren of Philadelphia and Buffalo's O.J. Simpson, with four rushing titles each. The next best streak (three straight years at the top) is a mark he produced from 1963-65 and shares with Van Buren and Earl Campbell.

Brown was born on February 17, 1936 in St. Simmons, Georgia. By the time he was a senior at Syracuse University, the NFL had discovered his many talents. Brown, who set a school rushing record that

When he burst into the open field, Jim Brown was usually gone. His 5.22-yards-per-carry average remains the best in NFL history.

© Fred Roe

If it was required, Brown could lower his head and break a tackle or scramble away from any attack. The game of football may never again see his combination of size, speed, and elusiveness.

would later drive Floyd Little and Joe Morris to personal heights as they pursued it, was an All-America in 1956 and a certain first-round draft choice in 1957. The only question was, who would get to him first? The Browns actually had their eye on Purdue quarterback Len Dawson; but Pittsburgh selected Dawson, and Cleveland reluctantly opted for Brown, the bruising 6-foot-2, 230-pound fullback.

Brown was that rare combination of size and speed. He was often as large as the linebackers that tried to tackle him and, clearly, faster than most. More than pure speed, Brown possessed quick accelera-

© Walter Iooss Jr./Sports Illustrated

tion at the line of scrimmage and the great field vision and instinct the truly great runners share. Unlike some college stars, Brown wasn't afraid of contact. Cleveland had featured six different runners in six previous years, including Dub Jones and Marion Motley, but Brown's first year, 1957, changed all that. He carried 202 times for a league-leading 942 yards and nine touchdowns. On November 24, Brown seared the Los Angeles Rams for 237 yards, a Cleveland record that only he would break. Not only did Brown set a team rushing record, he was named simultaneously as the NFL's Rookie of the Year and Player of the Year, an achievement that has never been equaled.

In 1958, he carried 257 times for 1,527 yards and seventeen touchdowns, and won the Most Valuable Player award. Brown's best season was 1963, when he carried 291 times for 1,863 yards, a phenomenal average of 6.4 yards per carry. In 1965, his final season, Brown won the MVP award again after recording league-high totals of 289 carries, 1,544 yards, and seventeen touchdowns. That kind of evidence suggests that Brown might have remained at his peak for several more seasons had he chosen to play. His health was always sound and he never missed a professional game for any reason, despite the great efforts opposing defenses made to stop him. Brown carried 200 or more times every season and also managed to catch at least 262 passes for 2,499 yards. In his final game, the 1966 Pro Bowl, Brown scored three touchdowns.

Ultimately, it was Hollywood that did what no defenders could. Brown landed a role in *The Dirty Dozen,* and, at the age of twenty-nine, decided to walk away from the game he dominated. He had nothing to prove to anyone on the field; Brown had reached the end zone a total of 106 times and gained 12,312 yards. He wasn't thinking of history and his place in it when he retired. Still, through the years, his quality has withstood the challenge of quantity.

Dick Butkus

Look at those eyes, the eyes of an assassin. Dick Butkus could intimidate opponents with his glowering gaze before the snap of the ball.

 HE WAS THE PROTOTYPICAL LINE-backer; a man who played the game in a terminally ill humor. Dick Butkus punished ballcarriers with a consistent resolve that is unparalleled in National Football League history. He was an old-school player who liked to play with a minimum of pads. The more cold and mud, the better. That is why the best college senior linebacker each year is honored with the Butkus Award.

"His intensity was incredible," says former Chicago Bears teammate Doug Buffone. "If I hit a guy, there was a ninety-nine percent chance he'd get up. If Dick hit a guy there was a good chance he wouldn't. He was that kind of player."

Butkus raised the art of tackling to a new high with hits designed not merely to take a man down, but to intimidate him. The highlight films are telling: Runner and tackler careen toward each other and, at impact, the offensive player crumples and falls backward as Butkus, legs still pumping, drives him to the ground with a shoulder. Butkus was so mean, he used his helmet as a weapon. He played only nine seasons, from 1965-73, but was named to the All-NFL team seven times and played in the Pro Bowl eight times. During that relatively short period, Butkus recorded twenty-two interceptions and recovered twenty-five fumbles. The one statistic, however, that would have underlined his savage temperament, forced fumbles, was not charted by the NFL in his day. Buffone estimates that it was close to one hundred.

In the 1960s, before Lawrence Taylor's pass-rushing skills changed the way coaches and players viewed the position, linebacker was not a glamorous spot to

As a middle linebacker, he was responsible for reading the field and moving to the ball. When he got there, someone usually paid the price.

© Neil Leifer/Sports Illustrated

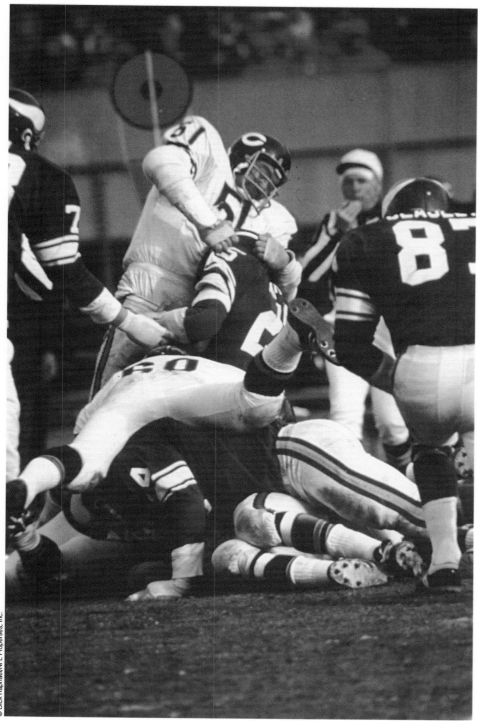

© Dick Raphael/NFL Properties, Inc.

play. Hard-hitting Chuck Bednarik of the Philadelphia Eagles, the last of the NFL's two-way iron men, had retired in 1962, leaving a void at linebacker at the time Butkus was beginning his rise to national prominence. Born on December 9, 1942, Butkus was an All-America at the University of Illinois his last two years there, and caught the attention of Chicago Bears coach George Halas. The Bears liked what they saw in the 6-foot-3, 245-pounder, who placed third in the Heisman Trophy voting. Chicago had made a deal in 1964 with Pittsburgh, trading its second- and fourth-round picks for the Steelers' first-round choice in 1965. That pick, the draft's third overall, went for Butkus. The Bears used the fourth overall to take running back Gale Sayers. They would both wind up in the Pro Football Hall of Fame.

Of course, the Denver Broncos of the American Football League recognized a brilliance in Butkus and made him a sizeable offer. Ultimately, the Bears won out and began seeing an immediate return on their considerable investment. Butkus ravaged the Cleveland Browns in his pre-season debut, making fifteen tackles and blocking a field goal. The Bears asked Butkus to follow in the footsteps of Bill George, who was one of the league's first great middle linebackers. In the regular-season opener, Butkus made eleven unassisted tackles and laid to rest any fears.

Certainly, he was blessed with size, but his greatest assets were strength and instinct. Butkus' speed was deceptive; though straight ahead he seemed almost plodding, his quickness usually delivered him to the ball on time. Sadly the Bears never made the playoffs during Butkus' tenure. Like many of his football peers, his career was cut short by a knee injury. By 1973, the pain in his right knee had become almost unbearable and Butkus retired. Today, Butkus is a popular and perceptive broadcaster with a gentle manner that belies the anti-social attitude he brought to the game. In his time, Butkus was the meanest, nastiest football player alive, which is to say, the best.

Wilt Chamberlain

IT IS SAFE TO SAY THAT FEW PEO-ple's sympathies ever laid with Wilton Norman Chamberlain. In a game of behemoths, he was a 7-foot-1, 275-pound giant among men. "Nobody," he said once, "roots for Goliath."

And though Chamberlain was easily the most dominant player the sport of basketball ever knew, he was almost universally underappreciated and misunderstood. His goatee, his menacing countenance in game situations, his flamboyant lifestyle, and his pride in himself left people with the impression that he was a self-indulgent superstar. Perhaps. At the height of his career, he built a $1.5 million mansion (when that kind of money meant something), and called it *Ursa Major*, the Latin version of Big Dipper, one of his many monikers. In truth, Chamberlain was supremely confident in his ability and wasn't afraid to speak with candor. The results backed him up.

Though he generally produced more points and rebounds than Bill Russell, Chamberlain performed in the shadow of the Boston Celtics' center who finished his career with a phenomenal eleven National Basketball Association championship rings. Yet, look at the numbers: When he retired in 1973, after fourteen seasons, Chamberlain had scored more points (31,419) than any player in history. To put that in perspective, consider that when Kareem Abdul-Jabbar broke his record, he needed a season's worth more games to achieve it. Chamberlain led the league in scoring on seven consecutive occasions, three more times than second-place George Gervin. His field

Wilt Chamberlain, forceful, snarling, arrogant, was always so easy to fear.

goal percentage is the best over nine seasons. Chamberlain's 23,924 rebounds still stand as the best total ever, and he led the league eleven times, for three different teams, in that category. He won four Most Valuable Player awards in 1960, 1966, 1967, and 1968. The numbers are simply numbing.

He was born on August 21, 1936 in Philadelphia, Pennsylvania, as one of nine children to a custodian of the Curtis Publishing Company. At fifteen, Chamberlain stood 6-foot-10 and already was vastly ahead of his competition. Even before he graduated from Overbrook High School, the NBA Board of Governors gave his eventual draft rights to the Philadelphia Warriors' Eddie Gottlieb. Chamberlain, according to National Collegiate Athletic Association rules, had to be content with a spot on the freshman team at the University of Kansas, but over the next two seasons he averaged thirty points and eighteen rebounds before accepting an offer from the Harlem Globetrotters in 1958.

The NBA knew he was eventually coming, and the players weren't particularly excited about it. Chamberlain's impact in 1960 was fairly incredible, since he became the first man to be selected the league's Rookie of the Year and Most Valuable Player simultaneously. Though Chamberlain was still a few years away from his physical peak, he was still stronger than any player in the league; he averaged 37.6 points and twenty-seven rebounds a game. And, while most big men developed moves that moved them toward the basket to take advantage of their bulk, Chamberlain's favorite shot was a ten-foot, fadeaway jump shot that was released above the basket. As opponents tried to force him farther and farther out of his range, Chamberlain developed some classic inside power moves and was soon a polished product.

The rookie that had pulled down fifty-five rebounds in a game against Boston was in full bloom two sea-

sons later when he averaged 50.4 points per game and became the first and last player to score 4,000 points—4,029 to be precise—in a single season. On March 2, 1962, Chamberlain scored 100 points against the New York Knicks at Hershey, Pennsylvania. A year later, Chamberlain sank eighteen consecutive baskets against Boston. Most of Chamberlain's points at this stage came on his monster slam dunk. He would hold his ground in the low post position, take the ball with one, huge hand raised aloft, and, practically at will, stuff the ball home. The Philadelphia franchise moved to San Francisco in 1962, but Chamberlain was traded back to the new franchise in Philadelphia, the former Syracuse team, three years later for three good players and a lot of cash. In 1967, the 76ers won 68 of 81 games, a professional record that would stand until the Los Angeles Lakers won 69 of 82 games four seasons later. Chamberlain was on that team, too.

Six years after he averaged fifty points a game, Chamberlain led the league in assists, with 702. This was a factor in the trade that sent "Wilt the Stilt" to the Lakers in 1968. His strength underneath the basket left him in perfect position to pass off to teammates Gail Goodrich and Jerry West. In 1972, the versatile Chamberlain sacrificed his scoring average (14.8 points) to give Los Angeles a rebound presence. His nineteen rebounds per game helped the Lakers to the NBA title, the second of Chamberlain's career.

When he took the ball to the hole, it usually went in, regardless of who tried to get in the way. Chamberlain was probably the most dominant player in NBA history.

Ty Cobb

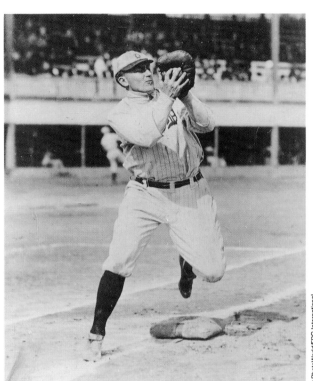

IT IS IMPOSSIBLE TO ACCURATELY compare baseball players from different eras, since the game has changed, albeit subtly, over the years. Today, pitching and power hitting benefit from a livelier ball. Back at the turn of the century, however, Tyrus Raymond Cobb dominated his era with skill, speed, and agility. He was, quite possibly, the shrewdest and most competitive player who ever lived. The image of his aggressive slide into second base, spikes flashing, is one that lingers. Cobb's personality was such that his teammates on the Detroit Tigers refused to share living quarters with him.

"Having to live alone," Cobb told famed sportswriter Grantland Rice, "I spent all my time thinking baseball, of plays I could make, of tricks I could try. Baseball was one hundred per cent of my life. I'd sometimes figure out a play, or a weakness, and then have to wait a month or a year before the chance came to use it."

He would take on opponents, or even teammates, but Cobb's greatest conquest was the record book.

As combative and competitive as Cobb was, his hitting stroke was a thing of beauty. Only Pete Rose collected more than his 4,191 hits.

© The Bettmann Archive

the first of three times, scored 147 runs, and knocked in 144 more. Cobb led the league five times in scoring, four times in runs batted in, and eight times in slugging percentage. In 1915, Cobb stole ninety-six bases, a record that stood until Maury Wills stole 104 in 1962.

By 1920, Cobb sensed a change in the game. "Well, the old game is gone," he told Rice as they watched Babe Ruth hitting batting practice balls out of Yankee Stadium one day. "We have another game, a newer game now. In this game, power has replaced speed and skill. Base running is about dead. They've all just about quit stealing; now they wait for someone to drive them home. I guess more people would rather see Babe hit one over the fence than see me steal second. Just watch the ball next year, they'll start juicing it up like a tennis ball, because Ruth has made the home run fashionable." Though Cobb was right, of course, his kind of game never went out of style.

Cobb's lifetime batting average of .367 is baseball's standard and may never be matched.

The left-handed batter played for twenty-four seasons, appeared in 3,033 major-league games, went to bat 11,429 times, and collected 4,191 hits. Until Pete Rose passed him in 1985, Cobb's hit total was the standard in baseball history. His career average of .367 endures, however, as the best ever. In 1922, eighteen years after he broke into baseball at the age of eighteen, Cobb hit .401. In some ways, that was more remarkable than the twenty-three consecutive years he batted over .300, or the .323 average he posted in his twenty-fourth and final season. There were also 892 stolen bases, a category he led the league in six different times. Though he was only an average center fielder, Cobb's speed usually neutralized any errors in judgment.

Cobb was born on December 18, 1886 in Narrows, Georgia, and was leading the South Atlantic League in hitting when the Tigers called him up and signed him to an $1,800 contract. The debut of the "Georgia Peach," on August 30, 1905, was in the form of a run-scoring double off spitballer Jack Chesbro. This, of course, came after a few nasty insults aimed at the New York hurler. "He came up with an antagonistic attitude," said Detroit teammate Sam Crawford. "He was still fighting the Civil War." Cobb explained himself this way: "If any player learned I could be scared, I would have lasted two years in the big leagues, not twenty-four. In legend, I am a sadistic, slashing, swashbuckling despot who waged war in the guise of sport. The truth is that I believe, and always have believed, that no man, in any walk of life, can attain success who holds in his heart malice, spite, or bitterness toward his opponent."

In his first full season, Cobb led the American League in hitting with a .350 average. Remarkably, he would finish first or second in hitting fifteen of the next sixteen seasons. In 1911, Cobb hit over .400 (.420) for

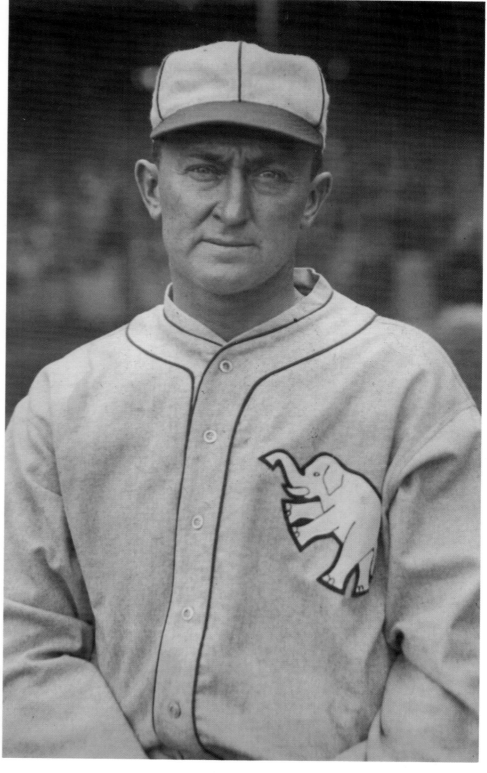

© PhotoWorld/FPG International

She was by consensus, the greatest female athlete in history. As Grantland Rice wrote, "She is an incredible human being."

© USGA Golf House

Babe Didrikson-Zaharias

SHE WAS, QUITE POSSIBLY, THE greatest female athlete in history. Babe Didrikson, the "Texas Tornado," dominated a quarter century of female sports in America. She was tall and slender, had powerful hands, legs like a football halfback, and a confidence in herself that was unshakeable. Her reflexes were very nearly perfect; there was nothing she couldn't do. Her track prowess was unchallenged; she once threw a baseball 296 feet, an Olympic record; her diving was polished and world-class; and her 100-yard freestyle swim was only one-fifth of a second slower than the world record. In 1932, she swung a golf club for the first time seriously. By 1935, she had it down to a science and was on her way to becoming

the best female golfer in history.

Mildred Didrikson was born in Port Arthur, Texas on June 26, 1914 and first found fame on the basketball court at Beaumont High School. She was spotted there by Colonel McCombs, who urged her to drop out of school and play for his Golden Cyclones. This suited the sixteen-year-old girl, whose love of athletics was balanced by a hatred of all things academic. It also opened the door for competition in tennis, swimming, and track and field. Soon, Babe (she was so named for her epic blasts on the baseball and softball diamonds) began appearing at the United States' most prestigious track and field events.

On July 16, 1932, Babe entered the national amateur athletic track meet in Evanston, Illinois and won

Above: Whether it was clearing a hurdle on the track or in life, or harnessing that raw power with a drive down a narrow fairway (left), Babe handled each obstacle with unsurpassed grace.

the women's team championship by herself. "It was one of those days in an athlete's life when you know you're just right," she wrote in her autobiography. "You feel you could fly. You're like a feather floating in the air." In a span of three hours, on a single afternoon, Didrikson won six gold medals and set four world records: in the high jump, baseball throw, javelin, and eighty-meter low hurdles. Her thirst for stardom was satisfied two weeks later in the Summer Olympic Games in Los Angeles. Babe won gold medals in both the javelin and the eighty-meter low hurdles, but was disqualified in the high jump and had to settle for a silver when her record was disallowed.

Didrikson was hailed immediately as a hero, something a Depression-stricken America needed badly. Grantland Rice, the famed sportswriter, was captivated. "She is an incredible human being," he wrote. "She is beyond all belief until you see her perform. Then you finally understand that you are looking at the most flawless section of muscle harmony, of complete mental and physical coordination the world of sport has ever known." Fame was fine, but Babe had to make a living. Two years after her triumph in Los Angeles, she was touring as a pitcher for the House of David baseball team. Vaudeville quickly followed, where Babe sang songs and played the harmonica. Bouts with professional basketball and billiards followed, but as it turned out, her true calling was golf.

Didrikson liked to say that her first encounter with the game came in 1932, when she was the guest of Rice at the Brentwood Country Club. In truth, it was her eleventh round of golf, going back to her days in Dallas. Her style, such that it was, wasn't pretty, merely effective. Babe held the club like a baseball bat and powered drives 250 yards. She was an abysmal putter, though, lacking anything resembling touch around the greens. Babe shot a ninety-five that day at Brentwood, but she was encouraged by praise from Rice. She won the second tournament she entered, the 1935 Texas Women's Invitational, and began to pursue a second career in golf.

After marrying professional wrestler George Zaharias in 1938 and changing her name, Babe honed her short game with tips from Walter Hagen and Gene Sarazen. In 1946 and 1947, she won seventeen consecutive amateur tournaments, including the 1946 United States Amateur and the 1947 British Amateur, the first American woman to ever win the latter event. In 1948, she turned professional and dominated the circuit by winning three U.S. Open championships, along with three Women's Titleholder tournament victories and four Western Open titles. Never bashful in the limelight, Babe helped launch the Ladies Professional Golf Association and was its leading money winner for four straight years. During her eight-year professional career, she appeared in 128 LPGA events and won thirty-one of them.

In 1953, Babe underwent the first of two complicated operations for cancer. A year later, she triumphed in the U.S. Open at Salem Country Club in Peabody, Massachusetts. Her 291 score was twelve strokes better than runner-up Betty Hicks. Two years later, she died with her golf clubs in her hospital room.

Joe DiMaggio

STYLE POINTS, THE BASIS FOR judging gymnastics, diving, and skating, don't count for anything in the meat-and-potatoes sports of baseball and football. Yet if they did, Joseph Paul DiMaggio probably would be considered history's greatest athlete. "Joltin' Joe" moved effortlessly around Yankee Stadium's vast center field, sometimes making it look almost too easy. He was the epitome of grace and, remarkably, played thirteen seasons without making a single mental error. Oh, he was once thrown out at second, trying to stretch a single into a double, but observers report that the umpire missed the call. DiMaggio's composure was legendary. Some people feel the highlight of his career came in 1947, when Brooklyn's Al Gionfriddo took away a potential game-tying, three-run home run with a sensational catch in the 1947 World Series. DiMaggio was already around second base when the ball he thought was gone was reeled in by Gionfriddo. DiMaggio actually kicked at the dirt just beyond the bag with a subtle motion, proving at least once that there were feelings running through that magnificent body.

DiMaggio's career statistics fail to explain his place in the game because he didn't play as long as Cobb, Rose, or Aaron; World War II cost him three seasons and he retired at the relatively young age of thirty-seven. Still, DiMaggio finished with 361 home runs and 1,537 runs batted in, a career batting average of .325, and one of the best-ever slugging percentages, .579. DiMaggio led the league in home runs, runs batted in, and batting average twice each, but the three-time Most Valuable Player had to be seen to be appreciated.

He was born on November 25, 1914, in Martinez, California, the eighth of nine children of Sicilian immigrants Rosalie and Giuseppe DiMaggio. He dropped out of high school to work the docks at Fisherman's Wharf in San Francisco. But, instead of joining the crew of his father's fishing boat, DiMaggio pursued a career in baseball, something his parents were predictably against. Joe's older brother, Vince, got him a tryout with the San Francisco Seals of the Triple-A

© UPI/Bettmann NewsPhotos

The DiMaggio follow-through on an Opening Day home run (above), the sliding technique into the bag (right), both were almost always flawless. More than anything, Joe DiMaggio was smooth.

© UPI/Bettmann NewsPhotos

38

Pacific Coast League, and at the age of seventeen, Joe made the team, playing shortstop in a few games at the end of the season. In 1933, he announced his presence to the baseball hierarchy with a terrific season. In 187 games, the rookie crafted a .340 batting average, based on 259 hits, and knocked in 169 runs. Included in the eye-opening package was a sixty-one game hitting streak, a tribute to DiMaggio's unwavering concentration and a delicious hint of things to come.

He was 6-foot-2 and painfully lean, though his frame later filled out to 193 pounds. DiMaggio had another great year in 1934, the year he was first discovered by the Yankees. Scout Bill Essick recommended that General Manager Ed Barrow make a bid on the prospect. This he did, for the bargain price of $25,000. As part of the deal, Barrow allowed DiMaggio to play the 1935 season in San Francisco, where DiMaggio had developed quite a following. After DiMaggio batted .398 and hit thirty-four home runs to lead the Seals to the Pacific Coast championship, he was ready for New York, where there had been only one pennant in the previous seven years.

Word of DiMaggio's exploits on the West Coast had reached New York, where he was viewed as a messiah of sorts. His first big-league season, 1936, was everything the Yankees hoped; DiMaggio batted .323,

hit twenty-nine home runs, and knocked in 125 runs. More importantly, New York won its first World Series since 1932, with DiMaggio getting nine hits. By his second year with the Yankees, the smooth right-handed hitter was the darling of New York. He hit forty-six home runs that season and knocked in 151 runs, both league-high totals.

In 1941, DiMaggio made history. Between May 15 and July 16, he hit safely in fifty-six consecutive games, a sustained effort some experts consider to be the greatest achievement in any sport. As DiMaggio passed Rogers Hornsby's National League record of thirty-three, then George Sisler's American League mark of forty-one, interest swelled across the nation. Wee Willie Keeler's nineteenth-century standard of forty-four fell and DiMaggio kept on hitting. Finally, on July 17 at Cleveland's Municipal Stadium, DiMaggio ran into the Indians' Al Smith and Jim Bagby. Ken Keltner saved Smith (who walked "The Yankee Clipper" once) by taking away two certain hits with great plays at third base. Bagby was on the mound for DiMaggio's fourth and final at-bat in the eighth inning. Shortstop Lou Boudreau took the bad-hop bouncer barehanded and turned a double play. Oddly enough, DiMaggio would go on to hit in the next sixteen games, a testament to his remarkable power of concentration.

In 1941, DiMaggio hit safely in fifty-six consecutive games, one of the greatest feats in all of sports' history.

A.J. Foyt

Over the years, A.J. Foyt won automobile races in virtually every venue, from the Indianapolis 500, to LeMans.

 AUTOMOBILE RACING IS A FAIRLY simple enterprise, if you can get past all the technical difficulties. Essentially, the man who runs harder, longer, wins the race. In many cases, however, it is that pedal-to-the-metal mentality that also leads to fiery crashes and, sometimes, even to death. All of this makes the accomplishments of Anthony Joseph Foyt, Jr., so remarkable, for he is the last of the great good-ol'-boy leadfoots. And, he lived to tell about it.

A.J. Foyt is probably the best example of the Great American Race Car Driver. He won the Indianapolis 500, auto racing's crown jewel, four times—an all-time record that includes three titles in a span of seven years. Foyt has tried his hand at stock car racing and found success, as well as world-wide ventures in various sports car venues. Like a number of racing champions, Foyt grew up with crankshafts, oil, and spark plugs. The transition to race car driving was inevitable.

He was born on January 16, 1935, in Houston, Texas, and by the time A.J. was three, his father, a

former racer and mechanic himself, had given him a bright red miniature race car. School held no particular interest, so by the age of seventeen, Foyt found himself racing motorcycles and jalopies. He ran on those dusty, by now forgotten tracks of the Southwest and he ran hard. Foyt was utterly fearless and, eventually, his skills brought him to Indianapolis. In 1958, at twenty-three, he was offered his first ride there. Foyt was a prototypical Texan: A solid 6-foot-2, 200 pounds, he cursed loudly when unhappy, which was often; most of all, he was an extremely bad loser. This last trait usually worked in the favor of the man they called "Super Tex."

Jimmy Bryan, a great racer in the 1950s, was impressed. "From the first time I saw him," he said, "I could see that he was stronger, smarter, and less scared than most drivers." This was Foyt's gift; he had the drive to succeed and the intelligence to know when to back off—most of the time, anyway. His first Indianapolis 500 was hardly a work of art. Foyt, the youngest driver in the field, lasted 350 miles before hitting a patch of oil and spinning out of the race. The following year, 1959, he placed tenth and, though he failed to finish in 1960, Foyt won his first United States Auto Club (USAC) national driving title, with victories in four of his last six races. That set the stage for 1961, his finest year ever.

Foyt started seventh at Indianapolis and worked his way through the field in characteristic, hard-charging fashion. He took the lead when Parnelli Jones' engine died, battling veterans Roger Ward and Eddie Sachs down the stretch. Sachs slipped into first place when Foyt stopped to refuel with twenty-five laps to go, but a worn tire sent Sachs into the pits himself and Foyt was the winner by eight seconds. He won three other races on the USAC tour and claimed another national driving championship. At twenty-six, Foyt was the youngest man ever to earn that dual distinction.

Clearly, his special place was the winner's circle at Indianapolis. He reached that hallowed ground four times, more than any man in history.

In 1962 he was headed for a second consecutive victory in the Indianapolis 500 when his wheel simply flew off the car. As it turned out, one of his mechanics had failed to tighten the bolts during a change. Foyt, ever the ungraceful loser, fired most of his crew after the disappointing race. In 1964, he won the Indy 500 for a second time, beating the crafty Ward by more than three miles. Things were going almost too well for Foyt at this point. Reality, in the form of a terrible, twisting stock car crash, came home to Foyt in January 1965. His brakes failed at 140 miles per hour and his car spun grotesquely through the air. Foyt broke bones in his back and heel and lost most of the skin on his body. Three months later, Foyt was driving a stock car at Atlanta Raceway. Facing death, he says, is a part of the game.

"It hurts when you lose friends," he has said. "Hell, we got feelings like anyone else. A good guy goes, and you want to park your car and chuck your helmet in the cockpit and walk away from it. But this is our business. Death and injury are part of the sport. We all live with it."

Foyt won at Indianapolis twice more, in 1967 and in 1977. Not content with auto racing's most visible trophies, Foyt followed his free spirit far afield. He won the 252-mile Nassau Trophy Race in the Bahamas, won the Twenty-four Hours of Le Mans with Dan Gurney, and made his mark in stock car racing, winning the Daytona 500. Foyt became the first man to win one million dollars in auto racing and built an impressive business empire. Winning, however, was his primary passion. One year, at a time when he was easily making a six-figure income, Foyt entered a $1,500 sprint car race in Terre Haute, Indiana. Starting last in an unfamiliar car, Foyt stormed through the muddy field and won the race. That same year, he blew his engine during qualifying for a stock car race in Milwaukee. Rather than sit out, he accepted a ride in another strange car, started last and, naturally, finished first.

Consistency, as in driving in 100 runs for thirteen consecutive seasons and in playing in 2,130 straight games, was Gehrig's hallmark.

© UPI/Bettmann NewsPhotos

Lou Gehrig

 ON MAY 2, 1939, LOU GEHRIG WAITED for New York Yankees manager Joe McCarthy in the lobby of the team's Detroit hotel. Later in McCarthy's room, Gehrig said, "I'm benching myself, Joe." For the first time since May 31, 1925, an incredible span of 2,130 games and nearly fourteen seasons, the Yankees played a game without their Iron Man. Gehrig was in a mystifying slump and it wasn't until seven weeks later that doctors discovered that he was suffering from amyotrophic lateral sclerosis, a disease that ravages the central nervous system. Gehrig's saddening end as a baseball player did nothing to obscure his enduring career. In fact, his struggle merely under-

lined the heroic nature of his achievement. Through sickness and health, stinging April cold, and the August heat of countless pennant races, Gehrig was there for the Yankees—every day. To put the record in perspective, consider that Steve Garvey of the Los Angeles Dodgers made a highly publicized run at the standard in the 1970s, but fell short after 1,207 straight games, the third-best total ever. Garvey would have needed nearly six more seasons of perfect attendance to break the record.

In some ways, Gehrig's durability overshadowed his sheer talent. Along with Babe Ruth, he was part of the most celebrated one-two punch in baseball history. In 1927, Ruth, Gehrig, Bob Meusel, and Tony Lazzeri were known as "Murderers' Row," and the Yankees might have produced the best season ever. They won 110 games and swept Pittsburgh in four games in the World Series. Though Ruth hit sixty home runs that year, Gehrig was second in the American League, with forty-seven. Lazzeri's eighteen placed him third, which demonstrates that Ruth and Gehrig were playing on another plane. Gehrig edged Ruth in runs batted in, 175 to 164, and in total bases, 447 to 417.

Gehrig hit .373 that glorious year and averaged a robust .340 for his seventeen-year career. Consistency was his hallmark in all respects; he managed to drive in 100 runs for thirteen straight seasons and led the league in that category five times. Gehrig's 1,990 runs batted in stand as baseball's third-best total, behind Henry Aaron and Ruth. Three of the six best single-season RBI totals belong to Gehrig, and his 1,888 runs scored signify one of baseball's best career efforts.

Henry Louis Gehrig was born in New York, New York on June 19, 1903 to poor immigrant parents. When he was accepted at Columbia University, his mother became the cook and housekeeper at the school's Phi Delta Theta fraternity house, and her husband later became the janitor. Gehrig was blessed with strong, sound values. The sense of responsibility his parents instilled in him soon became evident on the ballfield. After a wonderful career at Columbia, Gehrig stepped into the Yankee lineup in 1923, at the age of twenty. He developed into a player who could always be counted on when pressure entered the game. Gehrig's twenty-three career grand slams are far and away a record; and, in thirty-four world series games, he hit ten home runs, knocked in thirty-five runs, scored thirty, and batted .361.

On July 4, 1939, the Yankees and the baseball world bid farewell to Lou Gehrig. A total of 61,808 fans attended the game and ceremony that left everyone with a tight throat. Ruth was there, plus other alumni from the fabulous 1927 team. Gehrig, a largely silent man in his years in raucous New York City, spoke eloquently as millions listened on the radio. "Fans, for the past two weeks you have been reading about a bad break I got," he began. "Yet, today I consider myself the luckiest man on the face of the earth. I have been in ball parks for seventeen years, and have never received anything but kindness and encouragement from you fans." He continued for a moment, then added, "So I close in saying that I might have had a tough break. But I have an awful lot to live for." Gehrig died two years later, but his record of durability lives on; it may never be broken.

Gehrig also came through in the clutch; his World Series batting and slugging averages of .361 and .731 are among the best in history. Below, he crosses the plate after a ninth-inning home run in Game Four of the 1937 World Series.

Steffi Graf

AT THE PRECOCIOUS AGE OF NINE-teen, Steffi Graf produced a first in tennis: In 1988, she won the sport's cherished Grand Slam, then added an Olympic gold medal in the Summer Games at Seoul, South Korea. How she achieved the five-for-five sweep was just as impressive as the feat itself. Graf won the Australian Open, despite a troubling rain delay. She shattered everybody on the French Open's red clay at Roland Garros Stadium, then adapted to the Wimbledon grass and the challenge of Martina Navratilova to eventually dominate the London final. The United States Open, despite the distraction of world-wide media attention, was her stage, as were the Games at Seoul. Only four tennis players, two of them women (Maureen Connolly in 1953 and Margaret Court in 1970) ever managed to win a Grand Slam; Navratilova and Chris Evert, the dominant players of the 1970s and 1980s, never did. And to think that following her triumph the West German teenager promised to get better, adding, "I'm very excited that I achieved this now. It is something that not many people after me will be able to achieve, I think. It is amazing."

Graf was born on June 14, 1969, in Bruhl, West Germany. Her father, Peter, a former tennis player of some repute, helped insure her future greatness with constant direction and support. Graf was hitting tennis balls as soon as she could walk and won her first tournament at the age of four, bringing home a trophy that was six inches taller than she was. At twelve, Graf played in her first professional tournament. "It was in Stuttgart, and she played Tracy Austin in the first round, when Austin was at the top of her game," remembered photographer Dennis Klein. "Well, Steffi lost, but it was close. Either a close two sets or it went to a third. And I remember it so well, because afterward, she was so angry about losing. There was none of this stuff about feeling good for a good match against one of the top players in the world. She thought she should have won."

This kind of attitude carried Graf to eventual success on the women's professional tour, beginning in 1982. She would be accused of playing mechanically, without emotion, but that stern demeanor and undeniable relentlessness are the chief reasons for her invincible run of victories. Her big, powerful forehand, the hardest shot in the history of the women's game, did her talking for her.

She is the athlete of the nineties: large, powerful, agile. At the age of fourteen, Steffi Graf was dominating women twice her age. How good will she be when she reaches her peak?

The forehand is the centerpiece of Graf's game. It is the hardest shot in the history of women's tennis.

Her incredible 1988 year began with a win over Evert in the Australian Open final, she then rolled over Natalia Zvereva in the French Open final, and overcame a first-set loss to beat Navratilova at Wimbledon. That set the stage for the September U.S. Open in Flushing, New York. Graf's only two losses for the entire year were to her doubles partner, Gabriela Sabatini of Argentina—that is who she met in the final. Though Graf won the first set in fairly typical form,

6–3, Sabatini began to place her high-bouncing top-spin shots accurately; when Graf showed her only signs of nervousness with several missed forehands, Sabatini had evened the match with a 6–3 win in the second set. Sabatini made a terrific volley for a winner to open the third set, and suddenly Graf looked vulnerable. No matter, for she won the next eight straight points and fifteen of the next sixteen to put the match away. It was 6–1 in the third and decisive set and a crushed Sabatini explained, "Steffi's mentality was perfect." And though Navratilova had been upset in the quarterfinals by Zina Garrison and Evert withdrew from her semifinal match with Graf complaining of stomach cramps, her victory was untarnished.

So, too, was the gold she won at Seoul. It was the first time tennis was offered formally at the Olympic Games, and Graf was determined to make history. She met Sabatini in the final and, again, wore her down, running her from side to side with a variety of shots. Graf prevailed, 6–3, 6–3, in a match characteristically devoid of drama. She finished the 1988 season with a 72–3 singles record. The champion, who at that point had won more than $3,287,440 in her brief career, was asked about playing for her country with no purse at stake. "I don't think about the money," she said after the medal ceremony. "I wanted to win the gold medal. I care more about winning than about making money." Safe to say, she will be doing both for quite some time. In the first major event of 1989 and her eighth consecutive Grand Slam final, Graf won the Australian Open in straight sets over Helena Sukova.

© Bruce Bennett

Wayne Gretzky

The Great One, with his play behind the net and constant motion in the offensive zone, changed the way the game of hockey was played.

 ON AUGUST 9, 1988, THE EDMONTON Oilers and Los Angeles Kings completed the biggest trade in National Hockey League history and, from a monetary standpoint at least, the biggest in the history of sport. In exchange for fifteen million dollars, three first-round draft choices, and two promising young players, the Kings received center Wayne Gretzky and two of his Oiler teammates. The deal immediately invited comparisons with the 1919 trade that sent Babe Ruth from Boston to New York for $100,000. The Canadian nation was outraged and New Democratic Party House leader Nelson Riis was moved to say, "Wayne Gretzky is a national symbol, like the beaver. How can

we allow the sale of our national symbols? The Edmonton Oilers without Wayne Gretzky is like...'Wheel of Fortune' without Vanna White."

To put the trade in the perspective of the NHL, consider that at age twenty-seven, the "Great One" was the third-leading scorer in league history, with 583 career goals and a record 1,086 assists in only 696 games, over nine seasons. Before Gretzky, who won eight straight NHL Most Valuable Player awards, no one had won the award more than three years in a row—something Boston's Bobby Orr accomplished in the early 1970s. Gretzky had won an astounding eight straight Hart Trophies, to go with seven consecutive Art Ross Trophies as the league's leading scorer.

Canada. Soon, his grandmother Mary was helping him hone his shot by playing goaltender while sitting in a chair as Wayne shot pucks past her. At the age of eleven, Gretzky drew the eyes of the hockey world by scoring 378 goals in eighty-five novice games against older teenagers. As an amateur at S.S. Marie in 1979, Gretzky scored 182 points in sixty-four games before getting the call from Edmonton of the World Hockey Association. Gretzky, then eighteen, scored 104 points his first season and the next year became the youngest player to reach the fifty-goal plateau when the Oilers joined the NHL. He wore number ninety-nine in double tribute to his childhood idol, Gordie Howe. The consistently amazing numbers and honors followed.

"I'm really most alive on the ice," Gretzky says. "I go on the ice and just do my job. I'm relaxed. When I first came up, I had the pressure to prove I belonged. The critics said I was too young, too small, and too slow. I had to prove myself to my teammates and management. I didn't want to let anybody down. I want to be remembered as a guy who had some talent, worked very hard to develop it, tried to contribute to his team and to the game, a guy who won a few Stanley Cups. So far, I'm on track pretty good."

As many goals as he has scored, Gretzky is always looking for an easier shot on net. He amassed over 1,000 assists in only nine seasons.

Before Gretzky, Orr held the NHL single-season record for assists, with 102. At the time of the trade, Gretzky had broken that mark eight seasons running, including a numbing record total of 163 in 1986. Before Gretzky, Phil Esposito of the Bruins held the NHL single-season goal-scoring mark, with seventy-six. Gretzky destroyed that record in 1982 by scoring ninety-two goals, then added eighty-seven two years later. In all, Gretzky held forty-one scoring records on the NHL books when he changed uniforms.

There are other numbers that underline Gretzky's incredible talent: He reached the once-hallowed fifty-goal mark in only thirty-nine games, surpassing the fifty-goal, fifty-game mark shared by Maurice Richard and Mike Bossy. In 1984, Gretzky scored in fifty-one straight games, totalling sixty-one goals and ninety-two assists for 153 points, a record comparable to Joe DiMaggio's fifty-six game hitting streak. Beyond brilliance and consistency, Gretzky was a leader for Edmonton; the Oilers won four Stanley Cup championships during his tenure, and without him the prospects looked bleak.

Like many champions, Gretzky's vision of the game around him transcends his rather ordinary-looking (5-foot-11, 170-pound) body. "Gretzky sees a picture out there that no one else sees," said Boston Bruins General Manager Harry Sinden. "It's difficult to describe because I've never seen the game he is looking at. He's the only player I've ever watched who gives me the goose bumps." Gretzky laughs at this suggestion of omnipresence. "I concentrate, maybe like a doctor concentrates in surgery," he said. "I prepare totally. I know they said Ted Williams saw a different, bigger baseball than other hitters. Hockey is pretty fast. I just try to be a little quicker than the other guy."

Wayne, the first child of Walter and Phyllis Gretzky, was born on January 26, 1961 in Bradford, Ontario,

Florence Griffith-Joyner

Even before the 100-meter race was over in Seoul, South Korea, it was obvious that Florence Griffith-Joyner was the fastest woman alive.

© Tony Henshaw/Sports File

 SHE BURST ON THE SCENE AT THE 1988 United States Olympic Track and Field Trials in Indianapolis, Indiana with a shocking, one-leg white lace singlet, flowing black locks, and incredibly long, wildly painted fingernails. Those who confused Florence Griffith-Joyner's flamboyant style with substance were set straight at the Summer Olympic Games in Seoul, South Korea. She took home three gold medals, narrowly missed a record-tying fourth and left, on many levels, a lasting impression.

Florence Griffith was born in 1960—one of eleven children—and grew up in a housing project in Los Angeles, California. Running had always been her chief talent and, as the 1980s were ushered in, she began to become a dominant force on the world track level. Griffith followed her coach, Bob Kersee, to the University of California at Los Angeles and soon became the National Collegiate Athletic Association 200-meter and 400-meter champion. In 1984, Griffith won the 200-meter silver medal at the Los Angeles Olympic Games behind United States teammate Vale-

© Diane Johnson

It was Griffith-Joyner's belief in herself and the will to pass up lucrative appearance money that kept her fresh for the 1988 Summer Olympic Games.

rie Brisco. And then Griffith quit track for two years.

She worked as a bank teller by day and slowly built a clientele for her hair-braiding and nail-painting business in the evenings. According to Kersee, Griffith gained sixty pounds and a husband during this period. While Kersee married United States heptathlete Jackie Joyner, who would win gold medals in Seoul's heptathlon and long jump events, Griffith came to love Joyner's brother, Al. They, too, were married, and Al (himself a gold medalist in the triple jump in the 1984 Olympics) convinced his new wife to resume training for the 1988 Summer Games.

Griffith-Joyner destroyed Evelyn Ashford's 100-meter world record of 10.76 seconds with a 10.49 at the U.S. Trials, and came to Seoul as a threat to East Germany's Heike Drechsler in the 100- and 200-meter races. Griffith-Joyner contemplated the Games with a sense of history. She was trying to match the performance of countrywoman Wilma Rudolph, the seventeenth of nineteen children herself, who won the 100- and 200-meter races and ran a leg on the 4 x 100-meter relay. "Here's what sprinting is all about," Griffith said. "It's Evelyn Ashford chasing records set by Marita Koch and Marlies Gohr. It's Heike Drechsler chasing the record set by Ashford. It's me chasing records set by Drechsler. It's the wanting and the hard work that go into the chase."

Her first race was the 100-meter. Both Ashford and Drechsler were lined up in the blocks when the

starter's pistol cracked. By the fifty-meter mark, Griffith Joyner had moved out to a comfortable margin and a smile began to spread across her face. By the seventy-five-meter mark, her elegant and chiseled face was pure rapture. She crossed the line with a shout, raised arms, and the fastest Olympic time in history, 10.54 seconds, but the strong prevailing wind didn't allow the record to stand.

The 200-meter race was the one she really wanted all along. Griffith-Joyner started well, ran a strong curve, and kicked hard down the stretch. The final time was an unbelievable 21.34 seconds, which shaved .37 off the existing world record. Moreover, Griffith-Joyner was four yards ahead of the second-place finisher, Jamaica's Grace Jackson. She fell to the track, thanked God, and began a victory trot around the track. "I had no doubt I would win," Griffith-Joyner said later. "I passed up a lot of things before the Olympics; I could have made a lot of money. I said, 'I'll sit out and go for the real gold in Seoul.'"

As planned, Griffith-Joyner ran the third leg of the United States' 4 x 100-meter relay. Though Griffith-Joyner's handoff to anchor Ashford was sloppy, Ashford held off the East Germans and finished with a gold-medal time of 41.98. The U.S. coaches then surprised many observers by selecting Griffith-Joyner to run the final leg of the 4 x 400-meter relay. When she received the baton from teammate Brisco, Griffith-Joyner trailed 400-meter world champion Olga Bryzgina of the Soviet Union by two meters. At one point, Griffith-Joyner closed to within one meter, but Bryzgina held the advantage as both teams finished well under the existing world record.

Griffith-Joyner was only mildly fazed by the results in the relay race. "These days," she said, "have been a dream come true, plus more that I didn't dream. I know I said the 200 gold was the one I wanted, but last night I laid out all the medals, and I felt that the silver was the special one because of the team's trust in giving me the chance. That silver is gold to me."

© R.L.A.P.I./FPG International

Eric Heiden

The power of Eric Heiden came from those enormous, hard-to-believe thighs; they were an incredible twenty-nine inches around.

AT THE 1976 WINTER OLYMPIC GAMES in Innsbruck, Austria, a sturdy seventeen-year-old American named Eric Heiden finished seventh in the 1,500-meter speed-skating event and placed fifteenth in the 5,000. He had earlier turned down a berth on the United States world junior hockey team and might have wondered if he made the right choice. Four years later, at the Olympic Games in Lake Placid, New York, Heiden dominated his sport in a single competition as no other skater has, before or since.

As Heiden threw himself into the 1977 season, it became clear that he would not finish seventh, or even second, to anyone. He won the first Grand Slam in the sport's history, sweeping the men's world, sprint, and junior championships. "It was like a dream," Heiden said at the time. "All the time I was looking up to those guys, those Russians and Scandinavians, saying how good they were, and suddenly...it's me." As if to add emphasis, Heiden repeated the feat in 1978. In 1979, Eric and his younger sister, Beth, entered eight races in their respective world championships and won all eight. Eric retained his all-around and sprint crowns, giving him eight straight world championships. The highlight of his Oslo, Norway performance was a world record of 14:43.11 minutes in the 10,000-meter race and an all-time record total of 162.97 points in the overall standings.

The secret to the 6-foot-2, 188-pound Heiden's speed was the power he generated from his muscular twenty-nine-inch thighs combined with an ability to relax under the furious pressure of international competition. "It takes years of concentration to learn to relax while competing, but Eric learned fast," said United States coach Diane Holum, who won four Olympic speed-skating medals in 1968 and 1972. "He has everything a champion needs: a lot of talent, very good coordination, and a good mental outlook. He trains very hard and has the right mindset."

Too often, the emphasis is placed on a champion's physical talent. Heiden had all of that, but it was his resolve that kept him on top of the world for four straight years. He had been born in Madison, Wisconsin on June 14, 1958, and was forced to commute to the United States' only world-class speed-skating rink (until Lake Placid) in West Allis, Wisconsin, some one hundred miles away. His grim regimen of bicycling, weight-lifting, and running gave him the strength and power to succeed. Heiden came to Lake Placid as the favorite in the five men's speed-skating events, the 500-, 1,000-, 1,500-, 5,000-, and 10,000-meter races. "When they talk about five medals, it goes in one ear and out the other," Heiden said on the eve of his first race. "I think one would be nice." Fat chance. Wearing, appropriately enough, a gold-colored, skin-tight speed suit, Heiden rewrote history and, amazingly, won all five gold medals. Lidia Skoblikova of the Soviet Union won a total of six gold medals in speed skating, but she did it at the 1960 and 1964 Olympics, and Clas Thunberg of Finland won five golds in the Games of 1924 and 1928.

On February 15, 1980, Heiden won the 500-meter event with a time of 38.03 seconds. That was followed by an Olympic record of seven minutes, 2.29 seconds in the 5,000-meters the following day. The 1,000-meter race brought his third gold medal three days later and another Olympic mark, this one (one minute, 15.18 seconds) four seconds better than the previous best. On February 21, Heiden won his fourth gold medal with another Olympic record of one minute, 55.4 seconds in the 1,500. Saving his best for last, Heiden won the 10,000-meter race, skating the twenty-five-lap, 6.2-mile course in 14 minutes and 28.13 seconds. That broke the existing world record by more than six seconds and beat second-place finisher Piet Kleine of the Netherlands by nearly eight seconds.

Heiden's accomplishments were partially obscured by another miracle on ice, the gold-medal performance of the United States hockey team. History will show, however, that Heiden's Lake Placid Games represented the highpoint of the sport since it became an Olympic event in 1924.

When Heiden won his five Olympic gold medals in 1980, he dominated the sport of speed skating in a single event as no other skater had, before or since.

Gordie Howe

As a bruising forward for the Detroit Red Wings, Howe seemed to lead the NHL in stitches nearly every season.

 STRANGELY ENOUGH, IT TOOK A PLAY by Wayne Gretzky on March 1, 1988 to drive home the greatness of Gordie Howe. Gretzky, perhaps the greatest hockey player ever, fed a short pass to Edmonton teammate Jari Kurri, who lifted it into the Los Angeles net. It was the 1,050th assist of Gretzky's career and it broke the long-standing National Hockey League mark held by Howe. "It's a pleasure to congratulate you," Howe told Gretzky. "Thanks for letting me keep the record awhile. There's no one on earth I would rather see get the record."

And there was no one on earth Gretzky would have rather surpassed than his childhood idol; for until Gretzky, Gordie Howe was the most decorated player in NHL history. When he retired from the league in 1971, he left records for most NHL seasons (twenty-six), games (1,767), goals (801), assists, and, possibly, stiches (well over 500). Howe, a bruising forward with an extraordinary ability to handle the stick, was named to the NHL All-Star team twenty-one times. "Both on and off the ice, Gordie Howe's conduct has demonstrated a high quality of sportsmanship and competence, which is an example to us all," said Lester B. Pearson, Canada's Prime Minister in the middle 1960s. "He has earned the title 'Mr. Hockey.' "

The beginning was hardly so grand. Howe was born March 31, 1928 in Floral, Saskatchewan. His mother purchased his first pair of skates from a neighbor for $1.50. They were made for an adult, so Howe wore his street shoes inside them. Though there was no hockey history in his family, Howe was determined to become a professional and he practiced endlessly, flipping pucks and tennis balls (during the offseason) against any available wall. The tall, awkward twelve-year-old played goalie for the King George varsity in Saskatoon, but stopping pucks wasn't enough. "We won the city championship that year," Howe said, "but I didn't like playing goal. It was too cold standing there doing nothing on an open-air rink with the temperature below zero. I wanted to score goals, not stop them." His coach advised him to stick with goalie.

Howe, the fourth of nine children, ignored the advice of his coach and was eventually reassigned to defense, where he developed his skating and led his team to another title. In 1942, he impressed the Saskatoon Lions, an amateur team, and won a job at right wing. Naturally, they won the provincial midget championship with Howe playing a leading role. Meanwhile, he was working at construction jobs, digging ditches that helped develop those broad sloping shoulders and muscular forearms. After a failed tryout with the New York Rangers, Howe won a 1944 audition with the Detroit Red Wings at their training base in Windsor, Ontario. Manager Jack Adams liked what he saw and Howe was placed under contract. After a season with Omaha of the United States League, Howe was ready for the NHL.

At 6-feet, 200 pounds, Howe debuted on October 16, 1946 at Detroit's Olympia Stadium. Not only could he score, but Howe had the tenacity to survive in the rough-and-tumble league. During the first road trip of his rookie season, Howe collided with Montreal's Rocket Richard. Richard took a swing at Howe, who ducked before knocking Richard down with a shot to the jaw. Sid Abel, a Red Wings player, couldn't resist taunting Richard. "That'll teach you not to fool with our rookies, you phoney Frenchman," he yelled. Richard skated over to the Detroit bench and broke Abel's nose in three places.

Howe was built for the mayhem of the NHL and soon earned a reputation among opponents as "Mr. Elbows." His teammates just called him "Power." Howe teamed with Abel and Ted Lindsay in 1947 to form the famous "Production Line," which brought seven league championships and three Stanley Cups to Detroit in eight years. In 1952, at the age of twenty-four, Howe won the Hart Trophy as the league's Most Valuable Player. At the time, Adams declared, "Howe is the greatest thing that has happened to professional hockey in twenty years." Fifty years was more like it.

Howe went on to win the Art Ross Trophy—for the league-leading scorer—six times and rewrote the NHL record book. He retired from the Red Wings in 1971 after twenty-five sensational seasons. Retirement didn't agree with him, however. Two years later, his wife Colleen negotiated a contract for Gordie and his two sons, Marty and Mark, to play for the Houston Aeros of the World Hockey Association. For the first time in professional sports history, a father and his sons were part of the same championship team, as the Aeros won the Avco Cup in both 1974 and 1975. Gordie was named the league's Most Valuable Player in 1974, and Mark was Rookie of the Year. Howe moved on to the Hartford Whalers, where, at the age of fifty-one, he finished his second career in the NHL and appeared in the 1980 All-Star Game.

© Bruce Bennett

As a member of the Hartford Whalers, Howe proved he could still play professional hockey, even at the age of fifty.

© Bruce Bennett

The Golden Jet might have moved across the ice faster than any other hockey player.

© Manny Rubio

© Manny Rubio

Bobby Hull

 SPEED THRILLS, AND THERE WAS NO one faster on skates than Bobby Hull, the "Golden Jet" of the Chicago Blackhawks. Hockey—the fastest spectator sport involving men under their own power—is a game that demands elusiveness. Hull delivered; he was once clocked just under a dizzying thirty miles-per-hour without the puck. There was more than mere speed to Robert Marvin Hull, however. The perfect complement of raw power made the left winger one of hockey's greatest goal-scorers and most-feared snipers.

Hull's left-handed slap shot was monstrous and became the bane of National Hockey League goaltenders as he rose to power in the late 1950s. The blinding shot was measured at 118.3 miles-per-hour and stood as the singular trademark of Hull who, like the greatest champions, harnessed something more awesome and unwieldy than most mortals. The slap shot was deadly accurate; Hull could pick a corner of the net and guide the puck there. On the rare occasions that the goalie had all the angles covered, Hull would attempt to blast it through him. The results were fairly incredible: In sixteen NHL seasons, Hull scored

610 goals and added 560 assists in regular-season games and produced another sixty-two goals and sixty-seven assists in Stanley Cup play.

In many ways, Hull, with his flashy style, helped usher in the modern, more offensive age of hockey. Many hockey youths attempted to emulate his wicked shot, but none quite mastered it. Though today a fifty-goal season seems almost commonplace, the threshold had never been crossed when Hull took to the ice in 1965. He scored fifty-four goals for the Blackhawks that season, the first of nine times that he would manage the feat in his twenty-four-year career. Hull led the NHL in goals scored in seven seasons. There were other honors, too. He won the Art Ross Trophy, awarded annually to the league's leading scorer, three different times; the Hart Trophy as the NHL's Most Valuable Player twice; and the Lady Byng Trophy, symbolic of that rare combination of large scoring numbers and sportsmanship (Hull recorded only 823 penalty minutes in 1,474 games) once. For contributions to hockey in the United States, Hull was awarded the Lester Patrick Trophy. His consistent excellence was reflected in his All-Star appearances. He was voted to the first team ten times and second-team twice.

From the beginning, Hull's brilliance was evident. Born January 3, 1939 in Pointe Anne, Ontario, Canada, Hull blossomed into an impressive player by the tender age of ten. That was when some experts first predicted the phenom would grow into an NHL player. He progressed quickly through the Blackhawks' minor league system and made his Chicago debut in 1957, where he played through 1972. At an age (thirty-three) when most players had long since retired, Hull jumped into a second career as a player for the Winnipeg Jets of the World Hockey Association. His presence gave the WHA instant credibility, and Hull ultimately lent more than his handsome blond looks and good name to the venture. In all games with Winnipeg and, briefly, the Hartford Whalers, Hull scored 303 goals and made 335 assists. Hull amazed the hockey intelligencia in the 1975 season, when he scored an amazing seventy-seven goals. Even in his later years, despite fighting a chronic case of bursitis in the shoulder that supplied the power for his slap shot, Hull was a lethal force.

When it was all over in 1980, Hull had scored a total of 1,018 goals and made 999 assists. Hull and Gordie Howe are the only two players in NHL history to record more than 1,000 goals.

As fast as he was, it was Hull's lethal slap shot, the one that traveled upwards of 110 miles per hour, that left opponents breathless.

Magic Johnson

© Doug Mazzapica

It is safe to say that no man ever passed the basketball as deftly as Magic Johnson. Here, against the Phoenix Suns, Johnson spots a Lakers teammate under the basket.

 WINNING MAY NOT BE EVERYTHING, but it is often a telling yardstick with respect to character and talent. Earvin "Magic" Johnson, a 6-foot-9, 225-pound guard as good as his name, is a classic point of reference. In baseball, New York Yankee catcher Yogi Berra played on ten world championship teams, and in football, the Pittsburgh Steelers Chuck Noll won all four of the Super Bowls he coached in. Basketball's standard of excellence has always been Bill Russell, whose Boston Celtics won eleven National Basketball Association championships in his thirteen seasons as a player there. Based on the early returns, Johnson belongs in that select company. By the age of twenty-

nine, Johnson had already collected five NBA titles with the Lakers, a National Collegiate Athletic Association championship, and an Olympic gold medal.

Born on August 14, 1959 in Lansing, Michigan, Johnson always seemed to have a positive effect on the teams he played for. He was a rare hybrid of size and speed; an athlete equally comfortable trading elbows with big men under the basket, or working the periphery, waiting for the perfect moment to unleash a searing pass. As a freshman at Michigan State University, Johnson led the Spartans to their first Big Ten championship in nineteen years. Coincidence? The record the following year was 26–6, including a dramatic showdown victory over Larry Bird's Indiana

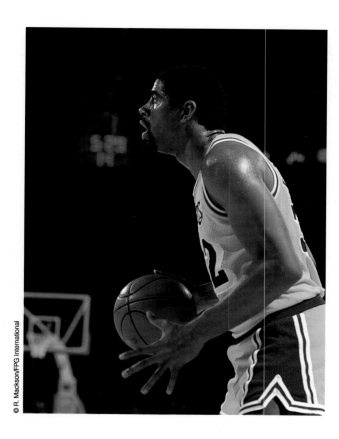

State University team in the NCAA final. Typically, Johnson was named the Final Four's Most Valuable Player. The professional scouts took notice, and Johnson left Michigan State at the age of nineteen. Johnson might have wound up with the Utah Jazz in 1979, but they had dealt away their first overall draft choice as compensation for free agent Gail Goodrich. Thus, the Los Angeles Lakers made Johnson their pick, and he responded with a terrific rookie season, including averaging eighteen points, seven rebounds, and seven assists per game.

Johnson's performance in the 1979–80 playoffs was truly of epic proportions. While averaging forty-one minutes a game, he scored his usual eighteen points and added ten rebounds, ten assists, and three steals to the equation. In the sixth game of the NBA final series against the Philadelphia 76ers, Johnson's versatility became a legend. With the news that 7-foot-2 center Kareem Abdul-Jabbar couldn't play because of a severely sprained ankle, Coach Paul Westhead opted for the rookie in the pivot. This was a troubling turn of events, since Abdul-Jabbar had averaged thirty-three points and thirteen rebounds against the 76ers. Yet, Johnson lined up opposite Darryl Dawkins. It wasn't even close. Johnson played forty-seven of forty-eight minutes and produced forty-two points, shooting fourteen-for-twenty-three from the field and fourteen-for-fourteen from the free-throw line, with fifteen rebounds, seven assists, and three steals. Dawkins, meanwhile, scored fourteen points and added only four rebounds as the Lakers won, 123–107. Johnson was named the playoff Most Valuable Player, the first rookie ever graced with that honor.

Two years later, Johnson led the Lakers into the playoffs again and emerged with another championship ring and a second playoff MVP award. Los Angeles won the title again in 1985, and in 1987 Johnson averaged nearly twenty-four points and twelve assists per game over the regular-season. Naturally,

he was named MVP, becoming only the third guard, after Bob Cousy and Oscar Robertson, to accomplish that feat. In the playoffs, the Lakers won their fourth title of the 1980s and Johnson was, of course, the MVP. Only Jerry West, Willis Reed, Moses Malone, and Larry Bird have ever achieved that rare MVP double. The following season, 1987–88, the Lakers took home another championship, marking the first time that it had happened in back-to-back years since the 1968–69 Boston Celtics. Johnson played another leading role, though teammate James Worthy was voted the playoff MVP.

Clearly, Johnson can do anything he wants to on a basketball court. Through nine NBA seasons, he averaged more than nineteen points a game, with 12,213 regular-season points. At the same time, his 858 assists in 1987–88 pushed him into third place on the all-time list, behind Robertson and Lenny Wilkens. Over the years, Johnson has brought new prominence to the "triple-double," a reference to achieving double-figures in points scored, rebounds, and assists. These well-rounded games best underline his value to the Lakers. Johnson remains only one of three players (Wilt Chamberlain and Robertson are the others) to produce 700 points, rebounds, and assists in a single season.

When Magic Johnson turns up the heat, there is no one more versatile in today's game of basketball.

Jones' psyche, not the golf course, was his greatest challenge.

Bobby Jones

 GOLF HAS ALWAYS BEEN ABOUT man's inability to master himself. Even Robert Tyre Jones, the sport's greatest legend, was not immune early in his career. The son of an Atlanta lawyer, Jones was born on March 17, 1902 and blessed with a broad-shouldered build and large, soft hands. Since the family lived just off the thirteenth fairway at the East Lake course, Jones was swinging a sawed-off club at an old ball by the age of five. He shot a seventy on

the East Lake layout at twelve, played in his first United States Amateur championship at the age of fourteen, and won the Georgia State Amateur title that same year. Jones had all the shots—the driver, brassie, spoon, and mashie—but the one thing he couldn't control was himself. Jones' biggest hazard was his temper, and it threatened to destroy his entire game. For seven years, he struggled with a burning desire to make every shot a perfect one. History suggests that Jones' withdrawal from the British Open in

1921, when he took fifty-eight shots for the first eleven holes, helped him face his personality on the links.

Finally, in 1923, at the age of twenty-one, Jones won his first United States Open title and set off on an eight-year wave of dominance that featured four U.S. Open championships, five U.S. Amateur titles, three British Open crowns, and one British Amateur trophy. Those thirteen major tournament victories stood as a record until Jack Nicklaus came along. Yet, one of Jones' accomplishments may never be equaled: his Grand Slam of 1930.

After his debacle at St. Andrews in 1921, Jones had returned to win the British Open in 1926 and 1927. His performance at Hoylake, England was just as impressive; Jones edged Macdonald Smith and Leo Diegel for the first leg of his improbable sweep. Jones took his first and last British Amateur title at the Old Course of St. Andrews and returned to New York amid the pomp and circumstance of a ticker-tape parade. The U.S. Open, his fourth crown, was achieved with a 287 at Interlachen Country Club in Minnesota. Then, in the fall of 1930, Jones defeated Eugene Homans in the U.S. Amateur, recording his fifth victory in that cherished event. The wags of the time called it the "Impregnable Quadrilateral," and Jones was immediately recognized as a golfing genius. He had won all four major championships of his day in a single calender year, though the U.S. and British Amateur competitions have since been displaced by the Master's tournament, he helped nurture the Professional Golfer's Association championship as Grand Slam events.

The secret of Jones' success went beyond his aggressiveness in competition to his ability to strike well-placed shots under moments of extreme pressure. Through years of practice, he developed a picturesque swing that sometimes looked almost too easy: there was the economical backswing, the mechanical thrust of the hips into the ball, and a perfect follow-through, consisting of hands held high and torso turned toward the target. Though he was by no means a large man, Jones got the most out of his body with a keen sense of timing. Once on the green, his legendary putter, Calamity Jane, usually laid matters to rest. Named for a character from the Wild West, the hickory-shafted club with a slight loft in the blade rarely disappointed Jones, even after the shaft had snapped twice and was bound with twine.

After 1930, he never again played in a championship tournament; after his celebrated sweep, Jones had conquered everything on golf's great landscape, including his temper. He left the game a great legacy with his course designs around the country. Jones helped engineer the course at August, Georgia that hosted the Augusta National Invitation in 1934, a tournament that eventually grew into the Masters. Even when he was confined to a wheelchair with a spinal disease in his later years, Jones' mental toughness was his greatest asset.

Jones, shown here driving on a municipal golf course at home in Atlanta, Georgia, pulled off the grand slam in 1930 at the age of twenty-eight.

Arms, legs, and tongue akimbo, Michael Jordan is the epitome of the muscular NBA as it moves into the 1990s.

© Sports File

Michael Jordan

BY ITS VERY NATURE, BASKETBALL IS a sport of specialization. There are quicksilver guards, muscular power forwards, and long, lumbering centers. All of them fill a functional role on a basketball team. Some have a marvelous shooting touch, while others rebound, set picks, or play tenacious defense. Michael Jeffery Jordan, the 6-foot-6, 200-pound guard for the Chicago Bulls defies such categorization. Arguably, there was never a better player at both ends of the basketball court. The Boston Celtics' Bill Russell, perhaps the game's best defensive player in history, was limited offensively. Likewise, Wilt Chamberlain's seven

consecutive scoring titles were balanced against inconsistent defensive play. Oscar Robertson was wonderfully well-rounded, but he lacked Jordan's explosive quality.

Born on February 17, 1963 in Brooklyn, New York, Jordan was playing for Laney High School in Wilmington, North Carolina when he first came to the attention of Dean Smith. The University of North Carolina coach successfully recruited Jordan. Instant gratification came in the form of a national championship. Though Jordan averaged only 13.5 points that freshman year, he was the Tar Heels' undeniable leader. After back-to-back College Player of the Year trophies and an Olympic basketball gold medal in the 1984 Los Angeles Games, Jordan was ready for the professional ranks a year early. Smith's disciplined system at North Carolina had effectively kept Jordan's incredible scoring ability under wraps, and he was the third player drafted in 1984, behind 7-foot Nigerian center Akeem Olajuwon and 7-foot-9 center Sam Bowie. It was Jordan, however, who averaged twenty-eight points per game and won Rookie of the Year honors. Jordan's second season was curtailed drastically by a foot injury, yet he returned ahead of schedule and eventually left the basketball world talking about his feats of versatility.

In his third professional season, 1986–87, Jordan had one of the best offensive years in history. He scored 3,041 points, a record for National Basketball Association guards, and became only the second player after Chamberlain to score more than 3,000 points in a single season. While he was averaging 37.1 points per game, Jordan found time to produce 430 rebounds, 236 steals, and 125 blocks. So brilliant was his offense that, in most cases, his defense was overshadowed. Though Jordan, a man of immense pride, became the first man in history to make more than 200 steals and block 100 shots, there was another standard he still hungered for. In 1987–88, Jordan scored another 2,868 points, and added 259 steals and 131 blocks. The experts were left with no choice; not only was Jordan named the NBA's Most Valuable Player, based on his league-leading average of thirty-five points per game, but he was voted as the Defensive Player of the Year as well. In an incredible year of honors, Jordan was also the All-Star MVP and the winner of the league's exciting slam dunk contest.

Like Elgin Baylor and Julius Erving before him, Jordan seems to routinely defy gravity as well as reason. His leaping ability and extraordinary hang time allow him to make several moves to the basket, some of them scintillating, long after mere mortals fall to

earth. Not only does Jordan have a serviceable jump shot, but once within ten feet of the basket, he usually winds up with a layup. Though most big scorers rest on the defensive end of the floor, Jordan is relentless. His 131 blocks were more than a handful of centers could accomplish, and in one game against the New Jersey Nets, he produced ten steals. Remarkably, this kind of end-to-end effort hasn't prevented Jordan from setting an example of durability. In addition to his gaudy numbers in 1987–88, Jordan played in all eighty-two regular-season games and led the league with 3,311 minutes played, something of a surprise, considering his relatively slight frame. In fact, Jordan was the chief reason Chicago became a regular in the playoffs.

Through 1988, Jordan was averaging 32.7 points per game. There is a strong possibility that when his career is over, Jordan may have surpassed Wilt Chamberlain's all-time best scoring average of 30.1.

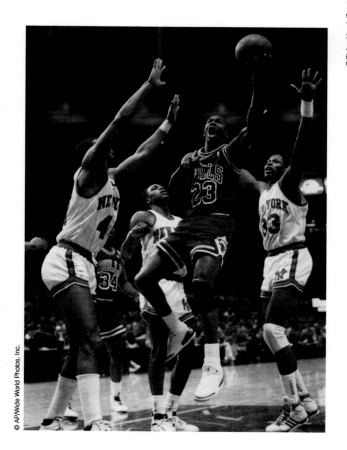

As spectacular as Jordan is on offense, he has recently been recognized as one of the league's premier defensive players.

Jean-Claude Killy

Through the fog at Grenoble, France, Killy prevailed to win three gold medals.

 IN A TIME OF TURMOIL AND SOCIAL awakening, Jean-Claude Killy was a rebel in his own way. While other skiers strained to lean forward, Killy pushed his sport out of the 1960s and into the future by sitting back on his skis. In typically contrary fashion, Killy seemed to defy all the conventions; he planted his pole far to the side when he set up for a turn, instead of close to the tip, and he anticipated the turn by twisting his upper torso well before he got there. It all added up to sharper turns and a quicker, more aggressive way down the hill. Even if he hadn't been

French, startlingly attractive, and a winner of three gold medals in the 1968 Winter Olympic Games at Grenoble, Killy might still have been a legend. Oh, but he was all of those things, and more.

In some ways, Killy was one of the first of the so-called ski bums, or, at least, a ski brat. He was born on August 30, 1943 in St. Cloud, France, and when his family moved to the resort of Val d'Isere three years later to start a ski club, Killy emerged as a natural. Killy's father was a former member of the French national ski-jumping team, and by the age of five, Jean-Claude was spending most of his free time on

© Fred Roe

In 1967 (below), Killy swept the alpine events at Kitzbuehel, Austria.

© AP/Wide World Photos, Inc.

the slopes. It was an amusing sight, this squat little fellow, so earnest in knee socks, shorts, and over-sized goggles. He won his first race, a cup offered by the vacationing Queen Juliana of Holland, at eight. Later that year, Killy won all three alpine events in the *Criterium des Jeunes*, leaving many twelve- and thirteen-year-olds in his wake. Killy, a small, timid, secretive child, enjoyed the notoriety his success brought. His style was a pastiche of the skiers he emulated as a boy, such as French Olympian Henri Oreiller and Adrien Duvillard.

"By watching many skiers and copying their styles, keeping some things, discarding others, I gradually developed a sense of what I wanted to achieve on skis—a style free of mannerisms, allowing for inde-pendent action of the legs, the lateral play of the knees and ankles controlling turns precisely and han-dling sudden checks and accelerations smoothly," Killy wrote in his autobiography, *Skiing . . . The Killy Way*. "I think most skiers lose the spontaneity they had as children. I didn't."

Trusting his instinct (he never once had a lesson), Killy progressed rapidly. After suffering a broken leg in Italy, Killy joined the French national team in 1960 and developed an immediate reputation for crashing. He attacked the course, attempting to sustain the straight-est, fastest line to the finish. The seventeen-year-old was learning, though. By 1964, Killy had qualified for the Winter Olympic Games at Innsbruck, Austria. Unrefined in the art of applying wax to his skis, undis-ciplined, and suffering from a case of amoebic dysen-tery, Killy placed fifth in the giant slalom and was eliminated in both the slalom and downhill.

Four years later, Killy arrived in Grenoble with a 1966 World Championship medal, a 1967 World Cup championship, and the heavy hopes of the Olympic host nation. Killy was attempting to equal the feat of Austria's Anton "Toni" Sailor, who swept the downhill, slalom, and giant slalom at the 1956 Winter Olympic Games in Cortina, Italy. Most observers felt it couldn't be done, and they were very nearly correct. Killy won the downhill by eight hundredths of a second, largely based on his charge out of the start and a clean per-formance on top of the hill. The giant slalom, his best event, was a great deal easier; Killy won by over two seconds. The slalom was a murky nightmare wrapped in a fog that wouldn't lift. Starting fifteenth, Killy could barely see the gates as he flashed through the course. Though he was leading after the first run, fourteen skiers were within a second of his time. Ski-ing a controlled and strangely disciplined race, Killy's second run was a testament to caution. Once again, his instincts didn't fail. Austria's Karl Schranz beat Killy's time by a half-second, but was later disqualified by the jury for missing a gate.

There will be those who discredit Killy's success at Grenoble. After all, Sailor won his three gold medals by extraordinary margins—3.5 seconds in the down-hill, 4.0 in the slalom, and 6.2 in the giant slalom—and he reigned twice as world champion. Still, Killy's accomplishments transcended the Olympic Games; he was a pioneer whose verve and style helped put skiing on the international map.

Olga Korbut

The genius of Olga Korbut: She balanced sheer athleticism with gymnastics' classic grace.

 THERE HAVE BEEN MORE SPECTACU-lar gymnasts—Rumania's Nadia Comaneci stunned the sport with the first perfect Olympic score (10.00) in Montreal in 1976—and more successful ones, as well—the Soviet Union's Nikolai Andrianov won seven gold, five silver, and three bronze medals from 1972 to 1980. Yet, never has there been a gymnast who single handedly captivated the world and sent the sport soaring to a new level. Olga Korbut, a 17-year-old, 4-foot-11, 84-pound sprite from the Soviet Union was that unlikely athlete.

As early as 1970, the Russian gymnastic braintrust was troubled by a lack of emotion in the performances of its athletes. Korbut, a fifteen-year-old reserve on the national team, would fill that void marvelously in two years. She was born May 16, 1955 and had first wandered into gymnastics in 1964, as a nine-year-old in Grodno, by the Polish border. Though she was tiny,

coach Renald Knysh liked her determination and sent her to Elena Volchetskaya, a member of the Soviet Olympic team. Five years later, Korbut successfully executed a backward somersault on the balance beam in the Soviet championships. The move had never been seen in competition, and many viewed it as dangerous, coming on the four-inch-wide beam. Korbut's exuberance was also seen as a threat to the staid state of gymnastics in Europe, where artistry and grace were held high over athleticism.

At the World Championships in 1970, Korbut won her first major title, the vault. Her big break came in 1972, when teammate Ludmilla Turishcheva slipped on the beam and lost her composure at the Soviet Cup. Korbut won the All-around Championship in dramatic fashion. That set the scene for her global debut in Munich, West Germany. In a sport where womanly performers like Turishcheva had dominated since the sport emerged in 1952 at Helsinki, Finland,

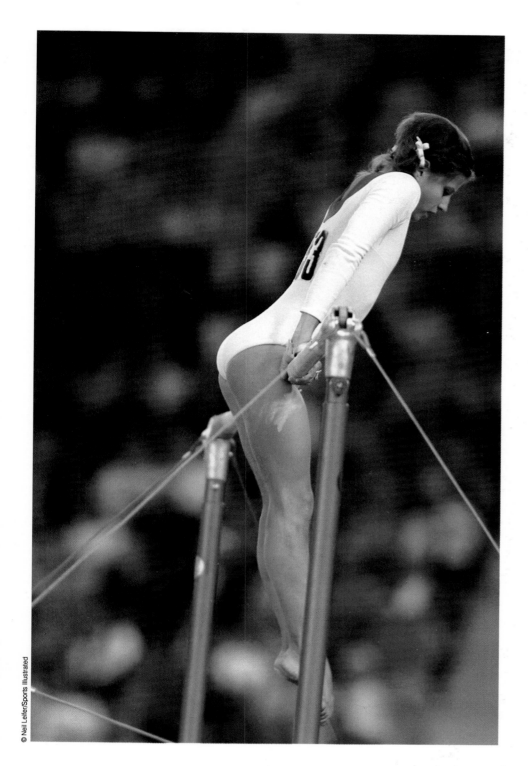

© Neil Leifer/Sports Illustrated

Korbut, with her elf-like appearance and daring moves on the uneven parallel bars, was a breath of fresh air.

Korbut was an Olympic favorite on the uneven bars, but it was a mistake that endeared her to the crowd and the hundreds of millions watching around the world. Halfway through her performance, Korbut stubbed her toe on the mat and the resulting lapse in concentration destroyed the rhythm of the program. Her previous lowest mark had been a 9.4 (out of 10), but when the 7.5 mark flashed up on the scoreboard, Korbut, like any other seventeen-year-old would, burst into tears; the up-close-and-personal lens of the camera didn't miss a thing. Korbut couldn't know it then, but she was instantly transformed into a star of global proportions.

Television, newspapers, magazines, and the people of Munich couldn't get enough of Olga. She returned the favor with a gold in the balance beam and another in the floor exercises, plus a team gold and a silver in the uneven bars. Korbut left Munich walking on air. She received the Soviet Union's Badge of Honor at a Kremlin reception, the youngest recipient of that award. That was the peak for the young gymnast. Korbut suffered a back injury, but returned to competition in time to earn a silver medal on the balance beam and another team gold in the Montreal Olympics in 1976. In an appropriate passing of the Olympic flame, Comaneci won the gold on the balance beam.

And though Korbut was succeeded by Comaneci in 1976 and Mary Lou Retton of the United States in 1984, she was the first gymnastic sweetheart; and the first love is the one you always remember. In 1988, Korbut visited the United States for the first time since 1976. "In the twelve years since I was here last, I've gotten tons of mail from Americans requesting autographs and pictures," she said. "So I knew I was remembered, but I didn't think to the extent that I now see."

It was the daring performance on the uneven bars at the 1972 Summer Olympics in Munich, West Germany, that caught the world's attention.

© AP/Wide World Photos, Inc.

So gifted is Carl Lewis that sometimes the world doesn't allow him any margin for error.

Carl Lewis

CHANCES ARE, HISTORY WILL VIEW Carl Lewis through kinder eyes than the harsh lens he finds trained on him today. In 1984, Lewis equalled the longstanding Olympic track and field record of Jesse Owens by winning four gold medals: in the 100- and 200-meter races, the long jump, and the 4 x 100-meter relay. However, in some ways, Lewis was considered a disappointment. Why?

"In 1984 and after, the media said, 'Carl Lewis is this, Carl Lewis is that,' " Lewis says. "More than make the public dislike me, it made the public misunderstand me. People wondered, 'What is Carl Lewis really like?' And if I'm not liked, there has to be a reason. Am I nice? Am I mean? Is it because I'm black?"

The answers aren't easily discovered, but Lewis offered a calculating and cool front to his fellow countrymen throughout the 1984 Los Angeles Olympic Games, and seemed at times to be a possessed man without a soul. At the age of fifteen, his elegant body had grown so quickly that he was forced to use crutches. Now, when he had the long jump comfortably in hand after his second jump, Lewis refused to take his third jump and try for the world record that might have been within his reach, opting to save himself for the 200-meter race and the relay. This action was received with disdain in a living-on-the-edge nation where performers who rarely take risks aren't considered entertaining. After the Olympics were over, Lewis tried to cash in on his success by recording

66

records and appearing in the movies. The public, however, wasn't buying.

As the 1988 Summer Olympic Games in Seoul, South Korea approached, Lewis' goal was an unprecedented repeat in all four events, a difficult act to follow, considering that no man in history had ever repeated as champion in even one of those events. The first test would be the 100-meter race, which he regarded as the greatest challenge. When his father, Bill, died after the 1984 Games, Lewis placed his 100-meter gold medal in his hands before he was buried. Two days before the showdown with Canadian sprinter and world-record holder Ben Johnson, Lewis' mother, Evelyn, dreamed that her husband returned to tell Carl, "It's all right. It's all right."

Ultimately, he was right, but when Johnson blew away Lewis and the rest of the world with an incredible 9.79-second time in the 100-meter final, Lewis looked like an also-ran. Johnson had sprung from the blocks in startling fashion and ran an unworldly race that broke his own world record. As Johnson crossed the line, he looked toward his bitter rival and raised his right hand and index finger aloft. Later, it was discovered that Johnson had been using illegal anabolic steroids, leaving Lewis and his time of 9.92 seconds (an American record) as the winner of the gold. Already, Lewis had surpassed the great Owens.

Next came the long jump, the event that Lewis had dominated for five years. True to form, Lewis won his fifty-sixth consecutive competition, but the fashion in which he won it was a departure from the usual *modus operandi*. Because of a scheduling peculiarity,

Lewis had run the second of two 200-meter qualifying heats only an hour before the long jump final began. With the 200-meter final the next day, Lewis could have easily saved himself after a few jumps as he did in Los Angeles. Though he led after three jumps, Lewis opted to jump a fourth time, even when officials forced him to make two jumps back-to-back after a controversy over the jumping order. Lewis' fourth jump was a monster—twenty-eight feet, seven and one-half inches—the day's best. Against the wishes of his coach, Tom Tellez, Lewis opted to jump a fifth and sixth time. Lewis slightly injured his right ankle on the takeoff board on the fifth, and his final jump fell well short of his best effort, but he had shown a new dimension to his character.

With his second gold medal in as many tries, Lewis faced the 200-meter race and his young protegé and teammate, Joe DeLoach. Two yards from the finish, DeLoach, running three lanes to Lewis' right, outkicked his training partner and made it to the tape in 19.75 seconds, .04 second ahead of Lewis. "I feel very good for Joe, I'm very proud of him," Lewis said. "I worked with him a lot, but when he had to get the job done, he got it done by himself."

Gone was Lewis' chance for another sweep, and when the 4 x 100-meter relay team was disqualified for an illegal handoff, he was left with two gold medals and a silver, a marvelous performance in retrospect. Somehow, the misfortune in Seoul left Lewis as a more sympathetic figure than he previously was. With the perspective of time, his achievement will be recognized for what it should be.

He is glib, dashingly handsome, and he can fly. History will judge the long jump to be his best event.

© Diane Johnson

Vince Lombardi

Lombardi demanded only one thing: your very best.

HE WAS KNOWN AS THE RUTHLESS disciplinarian who said, "Winning is not everything. It is the only thing." Yet Vince Lombardi moved his players like no other coach in professional football history. It was he who also said, "I hold it more important to have the players' confidence than their affection."

There are exactly sixteen coaches ahead of Lombardi on the all-time victory list for National Football League coaches, but not one has a better winning percentage. In ten seasons, Lombardi won 105 games, lost thirty-five and tied six, an unparalleled 74 percent success rate, directing the Green Bay Packers and Washington Redskins.

When Lombardi left his job as assistant coach for the New York Giants to become head coach and general manager in Green Bay in 1959, the one Giants player he brought with him was defensive back Emlen Tunnell, an eleven-year veteran.

"Those pep talks of his," Tunnell remembers. "I was thirty-six years old, and I thought I had a little sophistication, but when I heard those pep talks, I'd cry and go out and try to kill people. Nobody else could ever do that to me.

"I watched Vinny putting that team together, bringing in guys like Willie Davis, Fuzzy Thurston, and Henry Jordan . . . and I was sorry as hell I was so old. I would've given anything to be twenty-four again, because I could see what was happening. I could see the team getting better and better, getting filled with arrogance and proudness."

What was happening was the evolution of one of the greatest teams in sports history. Lombardi's Packers won five NFL championships in a seven year span, from 1961–67. The last two teams won the first two Super Bowls, underlining Lombardi's amazing record of post season success: 9-1.

In this day of one-million-dollar contracts and pampered stars, a Lombardi may never emerge again. He was tough on his players, he demanded punctuality (fifteen minutes early was too late), but he was fair. And, Lombardi got results.

"Coach Lombardi was so demanding and so short on praise that I would do anything to gain his acceptance, to get a kind word out of him," said Bart Starr, the Packers' quarterback for sixteen years. "I ignored injuries because he shamed me into it. He would walk into the training room and see a bunch of guys sitting around getting treatment and say, 'Who the hell do you think you are? You're not hurting; you're football players.'

"Most of all, he gave me self-confidence and that's because he was a super salesman. He had a knack of selling himself and his system and his ideas to football players. He was able to do this because he believed in himself and his system."

Lombardi was born in Brooklyn, New York, on June 11, 1913 and fell into football after failing at boxing and studying for the priesthood. He played guard at Fordham, where he graduated in 1937 and became one of the legendary "Blocks of Granite." Two years

later, Lombardi surfaced as the head football coach at St. Cecilia High School in Englewood, New Jersey. In 1954, at the age of forty-one, Lombardi joined the Giants at the request of Coach Jim Lee Howell. While at New York, he introduced the power sweep with its intricate pulling and trapping linemen. Five years later, Lombardi took the Green Bay job.

After that remarkable run of success, Lombardi stepped down. One season later, he was at it again, coaching the Washington Redskins. One year after that, Lombardi was dead at the age of fifty-seven, a victim of intestinal cancer.

"He treated us all the same—like dogs," said All-Pro defensive tackle Henry Jordan, who offers this classic Lombardi story: "One morning, we went out to the stadium, and it was pouring rain. I just took one look at the sky and I knew it was going to rain all day. We had a longer meeting than usual, figuring we'd never get out on the field to practice, and Lombardi was unhappy, walking around, wringing his hands and looking disgusted.

"Finally, he cut out pacing and looked up at the heavens and shouted, 'Stop raining! Stop raining!' And there was a huge clap of thunder and a flash of lightning, and the rain stopped. I'm a hard-shelled Methodist, but I've been eating fish every Friday since then."

In Green Bay, Lombardi took a team of middling veterans and fresh rookies and molded them into a group that dominated the 1960s.

At a time when the young Chinese divers articulated the movement toward athleticism and speed, Greg Louganis oozed style.

© AllSport

Greg Louganis

HISTORY'S GREATEST OLYMPIC DIVER was not always history's greatest competitor. It took the crucible of the 1988 Summer Olympics in Seoul, South Korea to bring out the tenacity in Greg Louganis, a sensitive man graced with sweetness in a sport that requires a killer instinct.

His emergence as a well-rounded human being is a story in itself. Louganis was born in 1960 and his parents, unmarried San Diego, California teenagers, gave him up for adoption to a commercial fisherman. Louganis was dyslexic, but suffered for years before the condition was discovered. He became addicted to drugs and alcohol by the time he reached junior high school. Diving was his rehabilitation and, ultimately, his salvation.

At the age of sixteen, Louganis won a silver medal at the Montreal Olympics in 1976. If not for the United States' boycott of the Moscow Games in 1980, Louganis might have achieved an unbreakable record of six gold medals for diving. As it turned out, he had to be satisfied with four. In the Los Angeles Games of 1984, Louganis became the first male diver since 1928 to win both the springboard and platform events, disciplines that require very different skills. The margins of victory (ninety-four points in the springboard and sixty-seven in the platform) were enormous in this enterprise where a twenty-point win is a landslide.

He had always prevailed on style and grace, but in the Seoul Olympics a new element entered his diving repertoire: guts. In the springboard preliminaries,

Louganis attempted a reverse two-and-one-half somersault in the pike position. His head grazed the
board as he spun by and his body crumpled on
impact. Several judges scored the dive a zero and
through the massive ache in his head Louganis wondered if he would even qualify for the finals.

"Greg grew teary-eyed at the thought of the lost
opportunity," his coach Ron O'Brien noted later. "He
thought it was the end of the road. I had to go out and
tell him he was still fifth (twelve qualify for the finals).
He couldn't believe it."

Louganis was given some temporary stitches for
the wound and walked to the board for the first of two
remaining preliminary dives. He thought of the 1979
meet in the Soviet Union when he had been knocked
unconscious after crashing into the ten-meter platform. If onlookers hadn't pulled him from the pool, he
would have died. He was unconscious for twenty
minutes. "I didn't finish that competition, so I wasn't up
there again right away," Louganis said. "That one was
easier to overcome because I didn't remember the
pain. It's harder when you're conscious, because you
remember."

Louganis completed the two dives successfully and
won easily in the finals over China's Tan Liangde, who
had beaten him several times earlier in the year. On
September 27, 1988 Louganis dived for the last time
in his career and, in many ways, his gold-medal performance in the platform was even more heroic than
the springboard.

Through six dives, Louganis was in third place and
the throbbing in his head wouldn't subside. Still, his
three-and-one-half somersault effort drew eights and
nines from the judges and bounced him back into first
place, ahead of China's Xiong Ne, a fourteen-year-old
acrobat who was half his age. Louganis' eighth and
ninth dives were effective but hardly spectacular, and
with one dive left, the Chinese teenager led by a single point.

The contrast in style between them was compelling.
Xiong Ne rotated so quickly through his somersaults
he was hard to follow. His splashless entries
impressed the judges. Louganis, meanwhile, was
more sleek in the air but the size of his well-muscled
body made clean entries difficult. Xiong Ne's final
dive, a three-and-one-half inward somersault, was a
good one. That left Louganis needing at least 85.57
points to become the first male diver to repeat as
Olympic champion at both levels. As Louganis
stepped to the edge of the platform, he reminded
himself that his mother would still love him, win or
lose. Louganis, not accustomed to the pressure of a
close contest, had saved his best and most difficult
dive, a reverse three-and-one-half somersault, for last.
It was virtually flawless—elegant and precise—and
the judges awarded him a 86.7 points, enough to
edge Xiong Ne by just more than a point.

When he saw the final scores, Louganis collapsed,
exhausted, in O'Brien's arms. "I competed well," he
would say later. "I kept challenging myself. Before the
Games, people expected me to do well, but it was
close. I'm pleased I came away with a good last dive.
I really needed it."

**Until the 1988 Sum-
mer Olympics in
Seoul, South Korea,
his competitive
spirit had been
questioned. On his
last platform dive,
he dispelled those
myths forever.**

Joe Louis

In 1951, Louis leveled Lee Savold with a sixth-round knockout to set up a rematch with Ezzard Charles.

THE POWERFUL NUMBERS OF JOE Louis' career as a heavyweight boxer fail to place in perspective his contribution to humanity. Though he won sixty-three of sixty-six career bouts, forty-nine by knockout, and reigned at the top of boxing's premier division longer than anyone in history, Louis transcended the entire sport. In 1936, after he had knocked out two former champions, the sage Damon Runyon wrote, "It is our guess that more has been written about Louis in the past two years than about any living man over a similar period of time, with the exception of Charles Lindbergh." Ordinarily, this would not be a strange turn of events in the United States, for the golden age of sports had produced many heroes in the 1920s and 1930s. The difference? Louis was the first black athlete to blaze across the consciousness of the American public. He was a symbol to both blacks and whites and was primarily responsible for opening sports to blacks in America.

From the beginning, Louis battled odds to win that role. Joe Louis Barrow was born on May 13, 1914, in a Lafayette, Alabama sharecropper's shack, the seventh of eight children. At the age of twelve, Louis' family moved to Detroit, Michigan, where Louis first encountered the ring. His mother Lillie hoped to keep him off the rough streets with violin lessons, but Joe had another idea. Dropping his last name so his mother wouldn't discover his secret, Louis used the money for his music lessons to pay dues at the Brewster Recreation Center. His first amateur fight in 1933 was a huge disappointment; Louis was knocked down seven times in two rounds by Johnny Miller, a United States Olympian in 1932. He quit boxing for six months on the advice of his stepfather. However, lured by the prospect of a professional career, Louis returned and won fifty of fifty-four amateur bouts over the next year, forty-three by knockout.

These were difficult times for a black athlete in America. Trainer Jack Blackburn told him, "The heavyweight division for a Negro is hardly likely. The white man ain't too keen on it. You have to be really something to get anywhere. The dice is loaded against you. You gotta knock 'em out and keep knocking 'em out to get anywheres. Let your right fist be the referee." It was advice that Louis took to heart.

On July 19, 1936, Louis met German Max Schmeling in a bout that had implications beyond the ring.

The fight came at the height of Adolph Hitler's popularity and was viewed by some as a test case for his ludicrous views of white supremacy. Louis, twenty-two, and by then a 6-foot, 218-pound undefeated fighter, understood the stakes, yet lost in a twelfth-round knockout, the first of his professional career. It was the last fight he would lose for fifteen years.

Exactly one year later, Louis met Schmeling in an anticipated rematch. "I'm scared," he told a friend before the fight. "Scared I might kill Schmeling tonight." It almost happened. With Yankee Stadium in New York swollen with 70,000 fight fans, Louis came out smoking and broke two of the vertebrae in Schmeling's back in the first round. A left hook followed by an overhand right ended the fight almost before it had started. In Louis' next twenty-five fights, only three men managed to go the distance with him.

One month later he stepped back into the ring and dispatched Jack Sharkey with a third-round knockout. On June 22, 1937, Louis met heavyweight champion James Braddock at Chicago's Comiskey Park. With 45,000 spectators looking on, Louis hit the canvas in the first round following a right uppercut by Braddock. By the eighth round, though, Braddock was in a daze. Louis' relentless punches to the body had taken their toll when an overhand right landed on Braddock's head and sent him down for good. Louis, at twenty-three, was the youngest heavyweight champion in history and only the second black man to hold the title after Jack Johnson.

For the next eleven years and 252 days, Louis kept his championship belt, a durability record that still stands for all of boxing's divisions.

Louis was a worldwide figure. Newspapermen created patronizing names for him like the "Brown

© AP/Wide World Photos, Inc.

Bomber" or the "Sepia Slugger" or the "Dark Destroyer," but Louis never complained or collapsed under the immense pressure on his broad shoulders. He embraced the World War II effort and spent his time away from the ring rallying around the flag. Louis returned in 1946 with an eighth-round knockout of Billy Conn, but in 1950 Ezzard Charles beat him on points. A devastating knockout by Rocky Marciano in 1951 ended Louis' career, but not his influence.

In 1947, ten years after Louis won the heavyweight championship for the first time, Jackie Robinson broke the color barrier in baseball with the Brooklyn Dodgers. Social change was painfully long in coming, but eventually it came, thanks to Joe Louis.

Louis knocked out Max Schmeling in 1936 (above) to blaze into the national consciousness. He held the heavyweight title for nearly twelve years. In 1951, ex-champion Louis defeated Freddie Bosheres (left) in the fourth round.

© PhotoWorld/FPG International

Connie Mack

HE BEGAN HIS MANAGERIAL CAREER in Pittsburgh, in 1894, the year Thomas Edison's kinetoscope was first unveiled in public. The movies, Connie Mack, and the face of the world had changed appreciably by the time he finished his last year with Philadelphia, in 1950. In between, there were fifty-three seasons at the helm of a big-league baseball club and enough wars and natural disasters in and out of the clubhouse to fill a lifetime. And that is just what Cornelius Alexander McGillicuddy gave to the game of baseball he loved so much: most of his life.

The gray numbers do Mack little justice; he managed more games (7,878), won more games (3,776), and lost more games (4,025) than any other man. He achieved nine pennants and five World Series championships, not to mention seventeen last-place fin-

Mack, the "Tall Tactician," was a fixture in the Philadelphia dugout for fifty years.

© PhotoWorld/FPG International

© PhotoWorld/FPG International

ishes. Yet Mack often went beyond his job description. He was a molder of men, and his subtle touch allowed great talent to emerge from players like Jimmie Foxx, Lefty Grove, George Earnshaw, Bobby Shantz, Mickey Cochrane, Rube Waddell, and George Kell. Mack was a *laissez faire* manager who understood the dynamics of a team. A quiet, nearly unflappable man, Mack left most discipline problems in the hands of the players. When someone loafed or was out drinking too late, second baseman Eddie Collins dealt with it, which won enormous respect for Mack's sensitivity and fairness.

Like many of baseball's best managers, Mack was hardly a natural; he began as a scrawny, 6-foot-1 catcher who hung on with three different teams for eleven years. Born in East Brookfield, Massachusetts on February 22, 1862, Mack quit school after the sixth grade to work twelve hours a day in the town's cotton mill. "It didn't seem so bad," he said. "Besides, we got an hour for lunch." Mack spent most of his spare time playing ball, and in 1884 the Meriden entry in the Connecticut State League offered him eighty dollars a month. One day (no one is quite sure when), McGillicuddy became Mack when a newspaper reporter claimed the name wouldn't fit into a baseball box score. Mack was not much of a hitter; he wound up with a career batting average of .245 and hit only five home runs. He survived on hustle and guile. Mack would distract the batter with his inane chatter behind the plate, call for quick pitches, and generally handle the pitching staff with rare skill. Since he wasn't blessed with great talent, Mack became a student of the game and mastered the pedestrian elements.

A fractured ankle was the break that sent Mack into managing. It was 1894, and Mack was appointed as the Pittsburgh player-manager for the final twenty-three games of the season. The thirty-two-year-old manager won more games (twelve) than he lost, but a seventh-place finish the following year and a sixth place finish the year after that left him unemployed in 1897. Mack was rescued by Ban Johnson, the entrepreneur who created the American League to compete with the existing National League. After a stint as manager in Milwaukee of the Western League, Mack was given the reins in Philadelphia, where the Athletics were viewed with skepticism. They succeeded, however, when Mack's charisma brought notable stars like Nap Lajoie and Eddie Plank aboard. The Athletics finished fourth in 1901, winning seventy-four games and losing sixty-two. The next season, with the addition of mercurial pitcher Rube Waddell, they won the pennant. Waddell, who led the American League in

strikeouts for six years running and totaled 131 victories in that time, was the ultimate test of Mack's legendary patience. In 1907, Mack finally gave in; Waddell was sent packing to St. Louis. "I just couldn't stand him any longer," Mack said. "I tried to get rid of players once I became convinced they would not cooperate, and Rube was certainly one of those. He gave me fits, but that fellow could really pitch."

Mack's 1911 Athletics were his best team. They won 101 of 151 games and took the pennant by thirteen and one-half games over the Detroit Tigers. Philadelphia prevailed over the New York Giants in a six-game World Series, bringing new credibility to the young league. Mack was scholarly and lent an air of dignity to the game that often featured bare knuckles and ceaseless profanity from the dugouts. For fifty seasons, he managed his beloved Athletics. As the years went by, Mack always maintained that he continued to manage because "if I did not, I would die in two weeks." On February 8, 1956, at the age of ninety-three, and less than six years after he managed his last game, Mack died.

Mack had the eternal respect of his players—he seemed to understand them, and it resulted in 3,776 career wins.

Rocky Marciano

PERFECTION IS THE GOAL OF EVERY professional athlete, though it is very rarely accomplished. Cy Young, the great baseball pitcher, managed to lose 313 games over his distinguished career; there were times when Cleveland Browns running back Jim Brown was stopped for a loss; even Boston Celtics center Bill Russell, the quintessential winner, found himself explaining a defeat on occasion. Rocky Marciano never, ever lost a professional heavyweight box-

ing match, a feat that stands as one of the greatest in sports. Only three boxing world champions moved through their careers unbeaten. Marciano is the only one from the twentieth century, although heavyweight Mike Tyson had his chance to approach that record.

American Jim Barry, who fought as a bantamweight from 1891 to 1899, finished with a 59-0-9 mark, and Irish lightweight Jack McAuliffe was 41-0-9 from 1884 to 1897. Marciano never drew with anyone; forty-three of his forty-nine victories were by knockout.

How many men go through an entire athletic career without suffering a defeat of any kind? Rocky Marciano, here (right) at his Grossinger's training camp, forged a spotless boxing record of 49-0. Whether it was Archie Moore at Yankee Stadium in 1955 (opposite page, above), or Roland LaStarza at the Polo Grounds in 1953 (opposite page, below), Marciano was up to the challenge.

He was born as Rocco Francis Marchegiano in Brockton, Massachusetts on September 1, 1923. Unlike many of his boxing brethren, Marciano was not an instant success in the ring; he came to boxing late in life after some success as a soldier in the United States Army. By the time he reached the age of twenty-four, Marciano had turned professional, but it would be six years before he was given the opportunity to win the heavyweight title.

Marciano was not a particularly big man; he stood just under 5-foot-11 and weighed a mere 189 pounds. His power came from a set of broad, well-muscled shoulders and powerful arms. His attitude of invincibility was steeled by the frustration that grew from fighting his way through a series of non-contenders to the top. In 1951, Marciano ended the marvelous career of Joe Louis by knocking him through the ropes and out of the ring at Madison Square Garden in New York. A looping right hand smashed Louis in the neck and left him defeated for only the third time in a sixty-six-bout career. Louis retired afterward, at the age of thirty-seven. On September 23, 1952, Marciano's climb was finally over. His manager, Al Weill, signed a contract

with champion Jersey Joe Walcott, and the two fighters squared off at Philadelphia Stadium. In the thirteenth round, seemingly out of nowhere, Marciano's right hand dropped Walcott to the canvas. It was the first championship appearance of the fist Marciano later named "Suzi-Q," and it would stand as the hardest punch he threw in his career. At the tender age of thirty, the "Brockton Blockbuster" was heavyweight champion of the world.

The obligatory rematch came eight months later in Chicago. By now Marciano's fame had spread, and he was the darling of boxing intelligencia. His first-round knockout of Walcott on May 15, 1953 was met with thunderous applause and the dawning realization that Marciano was a fighter of epic proportions. Four months later, challenger Roland LaStarza was stopped in the eleventh round in a championship bout. When Ezzard Charles emerged as the leading contender in 1954, Marciano gave him two title shots. The first was a close fight Marciano won on points, the second Marciano won in an eighth-round knockout. Don Cockell was a ninth-round victim in San Francisco in early 1955. Marciano's final championship bout, a brutal ninth-round knockout of Archie Moore on June 22, 1955 in New York, lent a certain symmetry to his fabulous career.

There are those who dismiss the competition Marciano faced during his professional career, but a man's place in time cannot be held against him. Marciano fought in seven world championship fights and won all of them—six by knockout. Throughout the history of sports there have been great athletes who lingered too long in their respective arenas. Motivated by money and ego, they finally reached beyond the grasp of their physical and mental tools. Heavyweight champion Larry Holmes, for instance, failed in a bid to match Marciano's great standard in a 1985 loss to Michael Spinks. Marciano knew when his time had arrived; his record of excellence may stand forever.

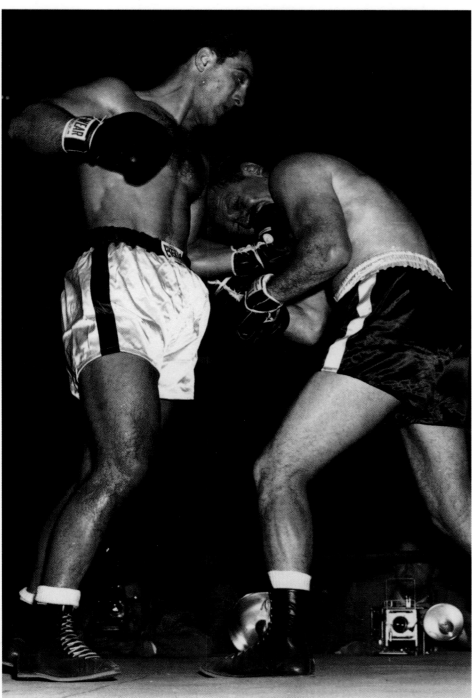

© Fred Roe

Willie Mays

Willie Mays, an unprecedented package of power and speed, hit 660 home runs and stole 338 bases.

 BASEBALL IS A LITTLE BOY'S GAME, and no one quite typified that like the "Say Hey Kid." Willie Mays arrived on the baseball scene in 1951, and for twenty-two seasons chased down fly balls in centerfield with reckless abandon, hit incredible home runs with seeming effortlessness, and ran the bases with verve and style. The 5-foot-10, 170-pounder had the gifts of speed and power. After he had finished with the New York Mets in 1973, Mays had accumulated 3,283 hits, 6,066 total bases, 660 home runs, 1,903 runs batted in, 2,062 runs scored, and 338 stolen bases.

Willie Howard Mays was born into a baseball family on May 6, 1931 in Westfield, Alabama. His grandfather had been a pitcher of some repute for several black teams around the Tuscaloosa area, and his father played regularly for a semi-pro team in Birmingham. Willie Jr. often joined him in the lineup. Mays was playing for the Birmingham Black Barons in 1950 when he was discovered, quite by accident, by New York Giants scout Eddie Montague. Only three years after Jackie Robinson's debut in Brooklyn, the Giants were one of the few teams sincerely interested in signing black players. Though Montague was in town to follow the Barons' first baseman, Alonzo Perry, he traveled back to New York and told manager Leo Durocher about the nineteen-year-old phenom he had seen. The Giants paid the Barons $14,000 and Mays was sent to Trenton, New Jersey and the Class B Interstate League. He batted .353 there in 1950 and, displaying a powerful arm, led the league in outfield assists. A year later, the Giants assigned him to Min-

© Fred Roe

Though he wielded one of the most potent bats in baseball history, Mays was even more exciting on the basepaths (right) or in the outfield (below).

© Fred Roe

neapolis of the American Association, where he hit .477 through thirty-five games. Tommy Heath, his manager at Minneapolis, told Durocher to keep Mays at his natural position in centerfield, because "he covered it like a tent." On May 25, 1951, Mays joined the struggling Giants and the would-be-savior promptly began his major-league career by making twelve straight outs. The Giants won those games, a tribute to Mays' bright outlook, said Durocher, who stuck by his young charge. Mays' thirteenth at-bat ended any creeping doubts; he turned around a Warren Spahn offering at the Polo Grounds with such force that it cleared the roof in left field.

On August 12, the Giants, an improving club since Mays entered the lineup, trailed the Brooklyn Dodgers by thirteen and one-half games. In one of the great charges in baseball history, the Giants won thirty-seven of their remaining forty-four games and caught the Dodgers down the stretch. In the final showdown of a three-game series, Bobby Thomson's "Shot Heard 'Round the World" lifted the Giants to the National League pennant. Mays' part of the bargain was a twenty-home run, sixty-eight-RBI season. And though the United States Army limited him to a total of thirty-four games the next two years, he returned in 1954 as a truly complete player.

Through ninety-nine games, Mays hit thirty-six home runs, but since the Giants were in another pennant race, Durocher asked for a higher percentage of singles. Mays, the consummate team player, obliged. Though he hit only five home runs over the last two months, Mays' batting average soared to .345, and the Giants won another pennant. Consistent power at the plate was one of Mays' hallmarks; he was first in the league in slugging percentage five times. He led all hitters with fifty-one homers the next year and led the league in that category four more times in his career, including 1965, when he popped fifty-two. Mays averaged thirty-five home runs between the ages of thirty and forty and even managed to steal twenty-three bases at the age of forty.

As sensational as his bat was, Mays was most exciting in the yawning green centerfield at the Polo Grounds and, later, at Candlestick Park in San Francisco. Most of the time, his basket catches at the waist sufficed, but when he had to run a ball down, Mays would do anything to get there. He dove, slid, and once, even took a ball in his bare hand. His speed and instincts allowed him to play an unnaturally shallow centerfield. Not only did this eliminate countless singles behind second base, but it forced Mays to make long, dazzling runs. The one people still talk about is a catch he made in the first game of the 1954 World Series against the Cleveland Indians. The image is frozen by time: the crack of the bat, Mays' quick whirl and sprint to the wall at the Polo grounds, his number, twenty-four, growing smaller and smaller as he catches up with the 440-foot smash, the ball dropping into his outstretched glove. It was the eighth inning of a 2-2 tie and Mays had bailed out Don Liddle and the Giants, who went on to win the game, 5-2, in the tenth inning, and eventually sweep the Indians in four games.

John McEnroe

© Bruce Bennett

McEnroe had all the shots: the gentle touch volley, the slicing backhand, the deft drop shot.

 HE WAS A REBEL WITH A BACK-hand, a product of the 1960s and 1970s, when America was in turmoil. John Patrick McEnroe Jr., was very much his own man, a left-handed gunslinger who berated referees that didn't measure up to his exacting standards. McEnroe was sometimes difficult to watch because he often treated himself with the same disdain. Underneath the bluster, however, was a creative, brilliant tennis master who played the game with uncommon grace. In a span of six years, McEnroe won four United States Open titles on the concrete courts at Flushing, New York and three more Wimbledon crowns on the unpredictable grass in London. In 1981, he seized the world's number-one ranking from Swede Bjorn Borg and essentially forced him into retirement with a classic victory in the U.S. Open.

Those in the profession who could see past the on-court bluster appreciated his artistry. "At his peak, John's style was to take advantage of any deficiency you might have and to put pressure on you," said Paul Annacone, a Davis Cup teammate. "John never gave you two seconds to catch your breath. He attacked any short ball, coming in behind immaculate approach shots. Look at what he did to Bjorn Borg, and Borg was a better version of Ivan Lendl. It was a privilege just to watch a guy at John's level. It was art, a fascinating game full of surprises and instinct, stuff that just can't be taught."

At 5-foot-11, 165 pounds, McEnroe was modestly built, but his catlike reflexes were evident even at an early age. He was born in Wiesbadan, West Ger-

many, but grew up in New York. McEnroe won the first of eight National Junior titles at the age of thirteen and achieved his first significant championship in 1976, winning the Orange Bowl tournament. A semifinal appearance at Wimbledon in 1977 announced his future championship status to the world. While at Stanford University, McEnroe won the National Collegiate Athletic Association singles title in 1978 and was named an All-American. McEnroe turned professional in 1978 and won several minor titles, including the Stockholm Open. He teamed with Peter Fleming in doubles and enjoyed even greater immediate success. At nineteen, McEnroe was a semifinalist at the U.S. Open and poised for a major breakthrough.

It all came quite naturally to McEnroe, who never put in the rigorous training hours of Borg or Navratilova. His keen sight and reflexes allowed him to place shots at will. His drop shot was a thing of beauty and his passing shots regularly skipped just inside the lines. His temper, the one that got him kicked out of the Port Washington Tennis Academy as a high-school junior, got all the attention, though. His fines over the years drew almost as much attention as his victories. "I'm not going to change," he told himself early in his career. "I'm going to show them."

In 1979, McEnroe and Fleming became the best doubles team in the world, winning at Wimbledon and the U.S. Open. By March 3, 1980, at the age of twenty-one, McEnroe became the world's top-ranked men's tennis player. In 1981, he won Wimbledon. McEnroe continued to dominate through the 1984 season, when he reached the finals of three Grand Slam events, winning at Wimbledon and the U.S.

© Bruce Bennett

Open. He had a two-set lead on Ivan Lendl in the French Open, only to falter. McEnroe's match record that year was an astounding seventy-nine and three. Through 1988, McEnroe's career winnings had reached $9,941,433.

In 1986, after losing to Brad Gilbert in the first round of the Nabisco Masters in New York, McEnroe left tennis to concentrate on his wife and two sons. "For the first four months of my layoff, I hardly even thought about tennis," McEnroe said later. "But around Wimbledon time, my interest came around a little. I realized I missed tennis, and I think tennis missed me. I needed that time off; I needed to step back and see the ways in which I was really a lucky person. Before all this, I had been dwelling too much on the negative, getting too resentful of people like the establishment and the media." His return seven months later was met with mixed results. In February 1987, McEnroe was beaten by his old foe, Borg, in a Toronto exhibition. The irony did not escape McEnroe, twenty-eight, who had convinced Borg, in compelling fashion six years earlier, that his time had come. At a party following the match, the two champions debated the issue of retirement long into the night. In a sense, the game had passed McEnroe by. Racket technology that gave lesser lights a more powerful serve and McEnroe's mental fatigue left him a shadow of his former self. Seeking the public's understanding he attempted a comeback that, by definition, could only fall short of the brilliance he once captured.

McEnroe's greatest weapon was his mind; he would hone in on an opponent's weakness and exploit it mercilessly.

For nearly ten years, Edwin Moses was unbeatable in his specialty, the 400-meter hurdles.

Edwin Moses

 THERE ARE LANDMARKS OF SUS-tained success throughout the history of sports that provide the scale for future accomplishments: Joe DiMaggio's fifty-six-game hitting streak, the Boston Celtics' eight consecutive National Basketball Association champion-ships, and Johnny Unitas' forty-seven straight games with at least one touchdown pass. For some reason, when those standards are invoked the name of Edwin Corley Moses rarely surfaces.

On August 26, 1977, Harald Schmid of West Germany won the 400-meter hurdles at the ISTAF Invita-tional in West Berlin. Moses was second. A week later,

on September 2, Moses won at Dusseldorf, West Germany in 47.58 seconds. He would not lose again for nearly ten years. Moses won 122 consecutive races, 107 finals, and fifteen preliminaries. No man ever dominated any event in track and field at so high a level for so long a time. If it were not for the United States' boycott of the 1980 Summer Olympic Games in Moscow, Moses would probably have won three gold medals in his specialty, an almost unheard of accomplishment.

After growing up in Dayton, Ohio, Moses went to Atlanta's Morehouse College where he first attempted the 400-meter hurdles at the Florida Relays in 1976.

He had always been a marginal hurdler, but as he applied the laws of physics to his sport, he began to flourish. For one thing, Moses took thirteen steps between the ten thirty-six-inch hurdles set thirty-five meters apart, while all other hurdlers took fourteen and fifteen strides. Moses won the United States Olympic Trials later in 1976 and finished the season with a gold medal at the Summer Games in Montreal. He graduated from Morehouse in 1977 and took a job with General Dynamics, but the demands of training proved to be too much.

As Moses' streak of successes grew, it almost diminished him. So routine were his victories that their majesty was chronically overlooked. Though he missed the 1982 season with pneumonia, Moses returned in 1983 with a World Championship gold medal in Helsinki, Finland, and a world record (47.02 seconds) in Koblenz, West Germany on August 31, his twenty-eighth birthday. There was another gold medal at the Summer Olympic Games in Los Angeles in 1984, and as Moses came to the starting line three years later in Madrid, eleven of history's twelve fastest times in the 400-meter hurdles were his.

On June 4, 1987, Moses lost to fellow countryman Danny Harris, an Iowa State athlete. Harris won with a time of 47.56 seconds, .13 of a second faster than Moses. Harris expressed his admiration for Moses, concluding, "You have to remember that I was in the sixth grade when his streak started." Moses responded with characteristic cool: "I'm glad it's over. I didn't have any bad feelings about the streak ending. It created new interest for our sport, and we need that. Now I can get back to concentrating on running fast instead of worrying about winning all the time. I'll be back because they've got me mad now, and I haven't been mad for years."

In 1987, Moses won the World Championships in Rome, prevailing in a blistering race that featured three men under forty-eight seconds—Moses (47.46),

Harris (47.48), and Schmid (47.48). "It's getting tougher and tougher to win," Moses said. "It took a lot just to get through to the semifinals. The event is very strong now. If I do say so myself, I've created a monster."

The monster jumped up and bit him at the 1988 Summer Olympic Games in Seoul, South Korea. At the age of thirty-three, Moses had won the United States Trials with a time of 47.37 seconds, the seventh-fastest time ever. "I proved age is not really a factor," he said. "That stunned everybody. They figured that the old man was either through or fading." It was to be his swan song. Moses failed in a bid to become the first athlete to win a gold medal in the running events over a span of twelve years when U.S. teammate Andre Phillips flew to a 47.19 first place victory, with Senegal's Amadou Dia Ba second (47.23), and Moses third (47.56). Though Moses had encountered an obstacle he couldn't hurdle, the loss put his extraordinary career into magnificent perspective.

Unlike mere mortals, who took fourteen or fifteen strides between hurdles, Moses took thirteen.

Martina Navratilova

saw Rod Laver play tennis. The left-handed Australian quickly became her idol, for Martina, too, was left-handed.

"After seeing Laver play I knew what world-level tennis was like," Navratilova says today. "I began having dreams about winning on Centre Court at Wimbledon or winning the Federation Cup for Czechoslovakia. They were the two greatest things a woman could do. It was the one dream you were allowed to have."

Under coach George Parma, a Davis Cup player for Czechoslovakia, Martina's game flourished. The modest facility at Prague's Klamovka Park was where the elements of Martina's powerful serve-and-volley game first came together. She commuted every day, a round-trip of an hour by train and streetcar. The family sacrificed five straight summer vacations so that Martina could travel to tournaments. She was eleven when Russian tanks rolled into Prague. A year later, Martina's cousin, Martin, defected to Canada, and her coach left for Austria. After tasting western civilization in West German junior tournaments, Martina began to long for the freedom and style of the West.

At the age of fifteen, Martina was invited to join the Sparta club, one of Czechoslovakia's most prestigious sporting associations. Even with this platform, she

From an overweight teenager struggling in a strange land, Martina Navratilova blossomed into the world's best tennis player. Fifteen million dollars later, Navratilova has made the serve-and-volley game her special niche.

AT THE AGE OF THREE, MARTINA Subertova found herself living in a single room of what had once been her mother's childhood estate along the Brounka River. From the window, Subertova, born October 18, 1956, could see the old tennis court that had now become a soccer field.

By the age of ten, Martina was playing soccer and hockey with boys and succeeding quite nicely when tennis suddenly became her life. Her mother, Jana, eventually married again, to a man she met at the municipal tennis courts in Revnice, Mirek Navratil, and Martina's name was modified into the present Navratilova. The young Martina used her grandmother's old-fashioned wooden racquets, and since they were regulation size, she needed both hands to wield them successfully. She was small for her age, but practiced relentlessly with her father, who convinced her she could become a champion. One night he took her to the Sparta sports center in Prague, where she first

consistently drew more acclaim from outside her country's borders than from within. Martina was authorized to compete in America in 1973, with Marie Neumannova as her chaperone. At the age of sixteen, Martina played well, showing promise for the future. At the same time she became fascinated with America and its cheeseburgers and 7-Eleven stores. The skinny kid they called "Stick," gained a quick twenty-five pounds. Bud Collins of the *Boston Globe* called her "The Great Wide Hope."

Two years later, Martina would beat Chris Evert for the first time in their celebrated rivalry; but, in their first meeting, Evert prevailed, 7-5, 6-3. After an eight-tournament run, Martina returned home. A year later, she made another tour, and the Czechoslovakian Tennis Federation was only too happy to pocket her $3,000 in winnings. After several clashes with the Federation, Martina flew to the 1975 U.S. Open and never went back. "I could look around and see that the Czech people weren't happy," she wrote in her autobiography, *Martina*. "There was a growing sadness. I began to realize that there was no room in the system for me to feel good about myself, for me to make decisions about my life. My life would never be my own."

At the age of eighteen, Martina took control of her life by defecting. She lost to Evert in the semifinals at Flushing, but she was free. Martina shed her extra weight and blossomed as a tennis player; she refined her game of strength, flexibility, and quickness, tamed her temperament, and chiseled a magnificent body from the one she had. Her big serve and strong groundstrokes left her as one of the game's dominant female players. In 1978, at twenty-one, Martina won Wimbledon for the first time, beating Evert in the finals, 2-6, 6-4, 7-5. Four days later, she was ranked first in the world for the first time, ending Evert's four-year reign. It would be another four years, however, before Martina would leave Evert in her wake and completely dominate women's tennis.

"We've never had anyone in tennis like her," said Pam Shriver, her doubles partner. "She's an athlete who takes care of herself, top to bottom. And her athleticism, her overall fitness program, will change the way women play tennis forever." Shriver was right. In 1982, Martina won Wimbledon again and returned to the All England Lawn and Tennis & Croquet Club for the first of what would be six consecutive Wimbledon titles. The total of eight championships (five over Evert in the finals) tied the record of Helen Wills, who managed the feat over a span of twelve years. Martina soon became the all-time leading money winner in the sport. Through 1988, she had won $14,058,199 overall. In 1984 alone, Martina won $2,173,556 and at one point, won seventy-four consecutive matches over eleven months and thirteen tournaments, the longest streak in history. Part of that streak was an incredible run of six consecutive Grand Slam victories, but because four of them did not fall in the same calendar year, she wasn't credited with the Grand Slam. That wasn't the point, however. "I guess," she said without sounding egotistical, "I have eliminated the unpredictability, the surprise."

Jack Nicklaus

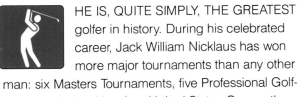

Over the years, the Golden Bear overcame the Arnold Palmer factions and became one of golf's most beloved personalities.

HE IS, QUITE SIMPLY, THE GREATEST golfer in history. During his celebrated career, Jack William Nicklaus has won more major tournaments than any other man: six Masters Tournaments, five Professional Golfer's Association titles, four United States Opens, three Tournament Players Championships, three British Opens, and two U.S. Amateurs. It all adds up to eighteen major championships (the TPC and U.S. Amateurs don't technically qualify) over a span of twenty-

three years, from 1962 to 1984. There were only two years when "The Golden Bear" didn't win or place second in a major tournament. He finished second eighteen times and third nine times. In ninety-two consecutive major appearances over that time, Nicklaus placed in the top ten sixty-seven times, an amazing record of consistency at the sport's highest level.

"The majors," Nicklaus once said, "are the standard historians use. They match you against the best in golf and place the most pressure on you to make

86

great golf shots. That's why I prize them above everything else."

Nicklaus is one of only four golfers, along with Gene Sarazen, Ben Hogan, and Gary Player, to have won each of the modern major championships at least once. Those legends all completed the set only once. To put Nicklaus' accomplishment in perspective, consider that he has won each three times. In 1972, he fell two shots short of holding all four titles during the same year. The last of Nicklaus' major titles was his most popular victory, coming as it did in 1986 when he was forty-six and thought to be well past his prime. Nicklaus entered the Masters at Augusta that year and his first three rounds were rather pedestrian; however, his reputation as the best final-round player ever was preserved on a Sunday. Summoning strength from the dogwood and azaleas of the Augusta layout, Nicklaus played the last ten holes in seven-under par to shoot a miraculous sixty-five for a one-stroke lead over Greg Norman and Tom Kite.

When Nicklaus finishes his career, the record book will show that he finished second behind Sam Snead with seventy-one tournament victories. Even more impressive are his winnings through the years, which total more than five million dollars. Partly through his rivalry with Arnold Palmer, Nicklaus helped golf secure its place among America's sports fans. As galleries began to swell in the 1960s, so did the purses. Palmer, who began his career seven years earlier than Nicklaus, was the first golfer to pass the one-million-dollar mark, but soon Nicklaus dominated that category. He followed Palmer over the one-million-mark in 1970, then became the first golfer to reach two million (1973), three million (1977), four million (1983), and five million (1987). Nicklaus led the PGA Tour in annual winnings eight times and, starting with his rookie season in 1962, recorded seventeen consecutive seasons among the annual top four money winners.

Nicklaus was born on January 21, 1940 in Columbus, Ohio and met his destiny ten years later when a professional golfer named Jack Grout gave him his first lesson. The chunky adolescent scalded the ball

© Diane Johnson

© Fred Roe

off the tee and developed a gritty attitude that served him well in United States Amateur match-play competition. Nicklaus first qualified for the prestigious event at the age of fifteen, and won it four years later, in 1951, the second-youngest winner ever. He won again in 1961, the same year he reigned as National Collegiate Athletic Association champion while attending Ohio State University. In 1962, Nicklaus turned professional and set his sights on Palmer, the favorite of the public.

As an amateur, Nicklaus had placed second to Palmer in the 1960 U.S. Open at Cherry Hills Country Club in Denver, Colorado. Now, he challenged Palmer again, this time at Oakmont Country Club in Oakmont, Pennsylvania. The four regulation rounds ended in a deadlock, with both men shooting 283. There was no question for whom the large gallery was pulling; Nicklaus, with a blond crewcut and stocky build, was seen as an overbearing, brash youth, while Palmer had been golf's leading light for several years. It was the more mature Palmer who succumbed to playoff pressure, however, and Nicklaus won his first major title by three strokes and a score of seventy-one, at the age of twenty-two. It would be more than two decades later, after an unparalleled run of golfing success, before Nicklaus would find himself in a similar position as Palmer.

Nicklaus took golf's major championships—the U.S. Open, the Masters, the British Open, and the PGA—and made them his own.

What a concept: A defenseman with breathtaking offensive skills. Bobby Orr was that man and he opened up the game of hockey in the early 1970s.

Bobby Orr

 THERE WAS A TIME NOT TOO LONG ago in hockey when the position of defenseman held little appeal. Small boys playing on frozen ponds in Canada dreamed of putting the puck in the net like Rocket Richard or Jean Beliveau of the Montreal Canadiens. Robert Gordon Orr changed all that. He was a rare hybrid: an offensive sniper in a defenseman's sweater. His offensive rushes into an opponent's end brought new glamor to the position and helped open the eyes of America to the National Hockey League. Orr simply controlled each of the 657 games he appeared in, playing the majority of the minutes, and carrying the puck more often than not. He could loop through an entire defense at will, or rag the puck seemingly forever when the team was short handed.

Orr was born in Parry Sound, Ontario on March 20, 1948, and by the age of sixteen, observers of the Ontario Hockey Association knew he was destined to be something special. Orr already had the speed, power, and finesse to compete on the professional level and he hadn't even finished growing yet.

The Boston Bruins struggled through the early 1960s, failing to secure a playoff berth for eight straight seasons. However, help was on its way. Orr's arrival in Boston did not bring any kind of sudden impact. Although he was named Rookie of the Year, the Bruins finished in sixth place in 1967, the last year before expansion. Boston needed some size and offense to go with its eighteen-year-old star. The Bruins' Milt Schmidt swung a deal, arguably the most one-sided in hockey history, that brought centers Phil Esposito and Fred Stanfield and right wing Ken Hodge to the Bruins from the Chicago Blackhawks.

Boston improved and in 1968 Orr won the first of eight consecutive Norris Trophy awards. Two years later, the Bruins were on the threshold of greatness. By now, Orr was recognized as one of the best defensemen to ever play the game. He was rewarded with an unheard of $400,000 contract, and his blond hair and blue eyes made him a cover boy in both Canada and the United States. The Blackhawks edged the Bruins for first place in the East Division in 1970, though both teams finished the regular season with ninety-nine points. "We have ourselves to blame," Orr said. "I can recall half a dozen spots where we either settled for a tie or blew a game we should have won. We're the best team. I know it, and the guys know it."

In the playoffs, the Bruins forged past the New York Rangers in six games, then dispatched Chicago in four straight. The St. Louis Blues, the West Division champions, never had a chance. The Bruins swept them in four games, and Orr scored the dramatic series-winner in overtime. Teammate Derek Sanderson fed Orr the puck and he moved in on goalie Glenn Hall. Just as Orr released his shot, St. Louis

defenseman Noel Picard tripped him. The image of a jubilant Orr, completely stretched out three feet above the ice, nicely framed the Bruins' first Stanley Cup in twenty-nine years.

There would be more successes. Orr won three Most Valuable Player awards, something defensemen weren't supposed to do, and earned the scoring title twice, thanks to his brilliance as the Bruins' pointman on the power play. In 1970, Orr managed thirty-three goals and eighty-seven assists, for 120 points. Then a year later, he produced thirty-seven goals and an astounding 102 assists, for a total of 139. Orr was named a starter on the All-Star team for eight consecutive seasons. He could shoot with the best, but his uncanny vision of the ice allowed him to pass the puck, which led to the bulk of his points. In twelve years, Orr would produce 270 goals and an amazing 645 assists, nearly one per game. There were other honors: twice Orr was named the best player in the playoffs, he won the Lou Marsh Trophy as Canada's top male athlete, and the Lester Patrick Trophy for his contributions to the game in the United States.

It was almost as if his talent was too great for his body to endure. In 1976, Orr became a free agent and signed with the Chicago Blackhawks. He played in the inaugural Canada Cup that year and was named the event's outstanding player. It was to be the last great flash of Bobby Orr. A sixth knee operation forced him to miss the entire 1977–78 season and after six games the next year, Orr retired on November 8, 1978, his knees no longer able to take him where he wanted. His time in the game was brief, but Orr's legacy persists today. He changed the game in both in the way it was played and perceived.

Orr won an astounding eight consecutive Norris Trophy awards as the NHL's best defenseman.

Jesse Owens

IT WAS 1936 AND ADOLF HITLER WAS approaching the zenith of his frightening stranglehold on Germany. He trafficked in racism, and what better forum to spread his vile seeds of propaganda than the Summer Olympic Games in Berlin? Though Paul Joseph Goebbels told the world that his blond Aryans would win all the medals available, in a mere forty-eight hours Jesse Owens, a proud black man, exposed the evil empire as a fraud.

With Hitler himself watching along with Goebbels, Himmler, Goering, and 100,000 Germans, the swift and graceful Owens ran and jumped his way into history. Using all of his 165 pounds and a pair of borrowed track shoes, Owens won four Olympic gold medals: the 100-meter, the 200-meter, the long jump, and the 400-meter relay race. He took the 100 in 10.3 seconds, an Olympic and world record that was later disallowed because of a trailing wind. The 200 was another Olympic record, at 20.7 seconds. Owens won the long jump in record fashion (26 feet, $5^{5}/_{16}$ inches) and later the team of Owens, Metcalf, Draper, and Wykoff ran a world-best 39.8 seconds in the 400-meter relay. And through it all, the crowd roared. When Owens received his gold medals, and smiled his broad smile, the empty box of the German leader foreshadowed history in a modest way.

He never ran against the stopwatch or other men, for that matter. Owens always remembered his mother's simple advice: "Do right, Jesse, and do good."

Born in the shack of an Alabama cotton picker in 1913, Owens developed a work ethic that would serve him well. He began running at Cleveland's East Technical High School in the 1920s and eventually moved to Ohio State University. There, he married at the age of eighteen and had a daughter at nineteen. "Nobody ever did it for me," Owens said. "Ever. I've never had an eight-hour day in my life, and in college is when I worked the hardest."

There in Columbus, Owens left his apartment at 6:30 a.m. and attended classes until 3 p.m. He worked out for an hour, then changed and worked full time, from 5 p.m. to 1 in the morning. Four hours of sleep later, Owens began the rigorous process all over again.

"Saturday nights after a track meet was his big time," said Larry Snyder, his track coach. "He was working, studying, and running, and it was good for him to bust loose once in a while."

The year before the Olympics, Snyder told Owens that even that small slice of relaxation was out. "All I had to do was tell him about it," Snyder said. "He didn't complain. Not even once."

The training routine expanded and on one, less-publicized day than his Berlin performances, Owens set six world records in one hour. At Ann Arbor, Michi-

© AP/Wide World Photos, Inc.

Three years before he made an eloquent statement for equality in Berlin, Jesse Owens was a sprinter for Ohio State University (opposite page). Owens, shown here taking the baton before the last leg of the 400-yard relay in a track meet against Great Britain (right), was one of the most versatile athletes in Olympic history.

gan, on May 25, 1936, Owens equaled the 100-yard record (9.4 seconds) at 3:15 p.m.; long-jumped 26 feet, 8¼ inches at 3:25; ran 220 yards in 20.3 seconds at 3:45; ran the 220-yard low hurdles in 22.6 seconds at 4 p.m. The two 220-yard runs were also ratified as 200-meter world records.

After the Berlin Games, Owens returned to New York and a ticker-tape parade on lower Broadway. Afterward, he basically ran for a living in exhibitions against cars, trucks, dogs, horses—anything that paid the bills. In 1948, twelve years after his Olympic triumph, Owens ran a 100-yard race in Barcelona, Spain at a searing 9.7 seconds. No matter that he was thirty-five, Owens decided he had run for the last time.

Owens understood his place in the world and maintained it with rare dignity. His eternal smile is the image that lingers even now. "You could be ever so tired," he said, "but the public is a funny thing. The moment you begin to think you are an ordinary human being with ordinary human being rights, the public can no longer look up to you. The public has made you, even though you have won something on your own. The public will not stand for prima donnas for long. There are many times when I don't feel like doing something—signing autographs or speaking for an audience or having dinner with people—but the public is not interested in explanations. You got to smile. You must."

Even when he was merely putting the golf ball, Arnold Palmer was charging. His style gave rise to an entire army of supporters. Over his glorious twenty-six-year career, Palmer won sixty-one professional tournaments. He's still competing on the Senior Tour.

© Diane Johnson

Arnold Palmer

 NEVER WAS A SINGLE ATHLETE more responsible for the sudden rise in popularity of his sport than Arnold Daniel Palmer. Golf had been a stylish, staid institution among the country club set since the 1920s and the days of Bobby Jones. Then along came hard-charging Arnie forty years later, hitching up his trousers and attacking the course with a new zeal. Suddenly, golf became fashionable for everyfan. If the charismatic Palmer hadn't stepped into the television arena as the 1960s began, he might have been created by an enterprising producer hoping for higher ratings. The long lens of the television camera caught every nuance of Palmer's muscular grace and helped lend the sport major-league status.

The style that remains Palmer's alone today on the Senior Professional Golfer's Association Tour was forged in Latrobe, Pennsylvania, where his father was a golf professional. Palmer, born on September 10, 1929, learned the game from his father, as well as all the grim maintenance chores a golf course requires. He was not a textbook golfer by any means; Palmer had rounded shoulders and crouched too much over the ball with his knees bent at a strange angle. A pair of tremendously powerful wrists allowed Palmer to overcome any technical shortcoming with sheer muscle and determination. He attended Wake Forest University, but did not make the immediate transition to the professional game. Palmer served a hitch in the U.S. Coast Guard until he was twenty-four. A year later, while employed as a manufacturer's agent in Cleveland, Ohio, Palmer won the 1954 U.S. Amateur. That prompted him to turn professional; his first victory followed a year later in the Canadian Open.

Palmer stood just under 5-foot-11 and weighed a modest 178 pounds, but he captured the imagination of golfers and duffers alike. He made his first impression in 1958, at the age of twenty-eight, when he won the first of four Masters tournaments in consecutive, even-numbered years. At Augusta National in 1960, Palmer erased an improbable deficit with three birdies on the last three holes to edge Ken Venturi by a single stroke. Later that same year, Palmer made one of the most memorable charges in golfing history to win his first and only United States Open. At the Cherry Hills Country Club in Denver, Palmer trailed leader Mike Souchack by seven strokes going into the final round, then birdied six of the first seven holes and shot a thirty on the front nine holes. Souchack was broken and Palmer coasted to a sixty-five and a two-stroke victory. "In looking back at Augusta and Cherry Hills, I won because I wasn't stopped by fear of failure," Palmer said a few years later. "It wasn't that I was playing all my shots brilliantly, but that I was ready to overcome the challenge of my own bad shots. I've always won boldly, or lost the same way."

Palmer winced when he missed a makable putt and Arnie's Army, a force that sprung up overnight, grimaced along with him. He flew his own personal jet to each tournament, accompanied by his wife Winny, and took home the important titles. In 1960, Palmer helped focus new American attention on the British Open, though he placed second by a stroke to Australian Ken Nagle at St. Andrew's in Scotland. A year later, Palmer prevailed at England's Royal Birkdale and defeated Dai Rees with a 284. He repeated in 1962 with a victory over Nagle at Troon, Scotland. Though Palmer never again made the trip across the water, his career record of three starts, two firsts, and a second has never been equaled for consistent excellence.

Palmer won sixty-one tournaments and an incredible $1,891,000 in his twenty-six years on the PGA Tour. He was a perennial favorite at the Tournament of Champions, and a winner three of the five years he played. Palmer was golf's first millionaire—in fact, he was one of the first millionaires in any sport. His personal services contract became the industry standard for all athletes, including rival Jack Nicklaus.

Today, the professional golf tour is populated by long, lean blond athletes who hit the ball a mile with mechanical precision that rarely excites the imagination. Arnold Palmer, meanwhile, is still the same, undisciplined golfer he always was. At the age of fifty-one, Palmer won the Canadian PGA, rekindling a love affair with the North American sporting public that still lingers.

Walter Payton, the man who rushed farther than anyone in NFL history, ran with the grace and unpredictability of a frightened deer.

Walter Payton

AT THE END OF HIS FINAL GAME, HE sat on the frozen Chicago bench, tears unabashedly rolling down his cheeks. The Washington Redskins had just submarined the Bears 27-13 in this January 3, 1987 playoff game on their way to victory in Super Bowl XXII, and Walter Jerry Payton was flooded with memories of a glorious thirteen-year career. "I've been fortunate," the halfback said later in the Chicago locker room as he took off the hip and thigh pads he had worn in every game since high school. "I've believed in myself and the Bears have believed in me, too. I'm sad it's all over, but it really hasn't hit me yet. Some day, this will all make sense."

Though there are those who maintain that Jim Brown and O.J. Simpson were better runners, Payton carried the ball more times (3,838) for more yards (16,726) than any man in National Football League history. It works out to nearly ten miles. His list of league records is staggering: seasons over 1,000 yards (ten), games over one hundred yards (seventy-seven), yards in a single game (275, versus the Minnesota Vikings on November 20, 1977), rushing touchdowns (110), receptions by a running back (486), consecutive seasons with 1,000 yards or more (six, tied with the Pittsburgh Steelers' Franco Harris), consecutive seasons leading the league in rushing (four, tied with Philadelphia Eagle Steve Van Buren).

He was called
Sweetness, but it
was largely a mis-
nomer; Payton had
the strength and
grit to run through
anyone.

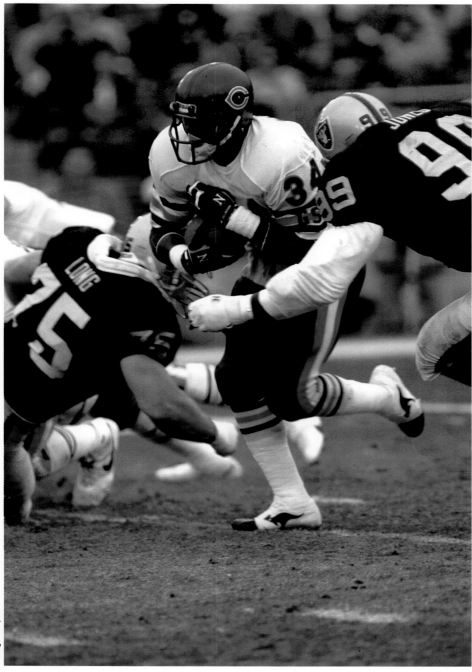

He was born on July 25, 1954 in Columbia, Missis-sippi and eventually enrolled at Jackson State Univer-sity, where he blazed onto the national football land-scape by scoring 464 points in four seasons, a National Collegiate Athletic Association record that included sixty-six touchdowns and assorted field goals and extra points. Payton gained 3,563 yards and averaged a monstrous 6.1 yards per carry. The Bears liked him enormously, but they chose fourth in the 1975 draft. Quarterback Steve Bartkowski was the first to go, followed by Randy White and Ken Huff, leaving Chicago to draft a franchise player well worth the wait.

At 5-foot-11, 202 pounds, Payton was an unprece-dented combination of speed, strength, and durabil-ity. According to Bears trainer Fred Caito, Payton's end was the means to his success. "He's got a big butt," Caito explains. In a sport where padding plays an important role, Payton was blessed with a formida-ble *gluteus maximus*. Not only did this help deflect would-be tacklers, but it gave Payton superior leg drive. It also allowed him to step higher than most running backs and spend more time in midair, lessen-ing the chances for injury. Payton's splay-legged style made him one of football's most picturesque players, as well as its most effective player over time. Although he was called "Sweetness" by his teammates, Payton was hardly a soft touch. He played the game like a linebacker, often seeking defensive players out; run-ning out of bounds to avoid a tackle was something he simply didn't do. Considering he went without consistent blocking until he reached the age of thirty, Payton's NFL records are remarkable. Recognizing this early in his career, Payton built himself a suit of armor in the weight room; he amazed teammates by regularly bench-pressing 390 pounds and lifting more than 600 with his sturdy legs.

His rookie season was a learning experience, for the Bears, anyway. Payton started only seven games and gained a modest 679 yards on 196 carries. For the next four seasons, however, Payton led the league in rushing and cleared the 1,000-yard barrier for six consecutive seasons. Only a strike by the players' union prevented Payton from stringing together eleven consecutive years over 1,000 yards. In the nine games played in 1982, Payton gained only 596 yards; however, the next four seasons he rushed over 1,000 yards per season.

On October 7, 1984, against the New Orleans Saints, Payton passed Brown's all-time record of 12,312 yards rushing with a six-yard gain in the third quarter. Payton finished the game with a total of 154 yards, and the Bears reached the playoffs for the first time in five years. The next season, 1985, Chicago was virtually unbeatable; only a loss to the Miami Dolphins marred an otherwise perfect season. Run-ning behind a talented and aggressive offensive line, Payton ran for 1,333 yards and caught thirty-seven passes for another 382 yards. Payton carried twenty-two times for sixty-one yards in Super Bowl XX, a resounding 46-10 victory over the New England Patri-ots. For Payton, it was another typically superb game in a superb career.

Pelé

HERE IS ALL YOU NEED TO KNOW about Edson Arantes do Nascimento: With all the world's modern athletes to choose from, the French sports magazine "*L'Equipe*" named him the Athlete of the Century. Jesse Owens, by the way, was a distant second.

He is known as Pelé, the best player ever in the most popular sport in the world: soccer. Between September 7, 1956 and October 2, 1974, the Brazilian forward scored 1,285 goals. The 1,000th came on a penalty kick for his team, Santos, in Maracana Stadium, in Rio de Janeiro, on November 19, 1969—in his 909th first-division match.

Born in Bauru, Brazil on October 23, 1940, all Pelé ever wanted was to be like his father, Dondinho, a second-division soccer player. "To me," Pelé says, "he was a very nice player. He make a lot of goal. He still have one record in Brazil because in one game he make five goal by head. I want very much to be like him as a boy. I remember a picture of many people carrying my father off the field on their shoulders after he win once with goal late in the game."

His mother, Celeste do Nascimento, did not want another footballer (as they are called around most of the world) in the family. Still, Dondinho prevailed. For fifteen years in Bauru, Pelé developed an almost

Twelve years after his World Cup debut in Sweden, Pelé still carried Brazil's colors proudly and elegantly in the 1970 final against Italy (below).

© Jan Collsico/AllSport

Early in life, Pelé wanted nothing but to follow in his father's footsteps. Later, his leading example would captivate the world of soccer.

© Fred Roe

unnatural feeling for the game. He dropped out of school in fourth grade, for soccer was his only love. Pelé played endlessly in loosely organized street games, called *peladas*, the source of his nickname. At the age of eleven, Pelé led Ameriquinha to successive championships in the Infanto Juvenil league. He was lean, but possessed endless energy and unique skill for one so young. Valdemar De Brito, a former national team player for Brazil, signed Pelé to a spot on Bauru's junior team, Baquinho. After three regional championships and forty goals in fifteen games, De Brito knew Pelé was destined for greatness.

At the age of fourteen, weighing all of one hundred and three pounds, Pelé traveled 300 miles to Santos, his cardboard suitcase filled with bread and bananas. He impressed team officials and signed a future contract before returning briefly to Bauru. A year later, on September 7, 1956, Pelé played in his first regular first-division game, against Santo Andre. He entered the game as a substitute; moments later he took a pass in front of the net, deftly eluded a defender and drilled a heavy shot into the corner of the net. Pelé played only sparingly in his first year, learning the intricacies of professional soccer. In 1957, he got his first start, against Sao Paulo FC, and responded with a terrific goal in a 3-1 win. He was suddenly discovered by the sporting press and proclaimed, correctly, as a genius.

Pelé finished the season with sixty-five goals, thirty-six in league matches. A fifteen-year-old had broken the equivalent of Babe Ruth's home run record in his first year as a professional. Greater things were in store.

"I do not think I was prepared for what happened in 1958," Pelé says. "I have no idea before of how my life would change in that year. It all happen very fast. It seemed like a dream. When I think back now, I do not remember very much of what happened. I know the goal against Wales was maybe the most important of my life. Then, when we beat France, I become very famous all over the world."

What happened at the World Cup in Sweden was a canonization of sorts. Though Brazil was the favorite to win, no one expected a child to lead them. The Brazilian team had reached three consecutive Cup finals, only to lose, which left many people wondering about their collective character. Austria fell 3-0, followed by Brazil's 2-0 win over Russia. Wales, Brazil's quarterfinal opponent, had a tough defense, a unit that did not crack for sixty-six minutes. It was Pelé who broke a scoreless deadlock, with an admittedly lucky shot off of a defender's boot. Pelé scored three goals against France to vault Brazil to the final against Sweden. With Brazil leading 2-1, Pelé scored the tournament's most memorable goal. He trapped the ball with his thigh in the Swedish penalty area, let it drop to the crook of his ankle, and in the same motion loped over his own head and that of a frozen defender and snapped a rocket into the net. That gave Brazil the Cup and Pelé a world stage.

There would be more spectacular goals for Pelé and success for Santos and the Brazilian national team. Brazil repeated as champion in the 1962 World Cup in Chile, but lost in 1966 when Pelé suffered a knee injury after repeated fouls against him. Santos, meanwhile, won a number of world titles and became one of soccer's most formidable touring clubs. Eight months after he announced his retirement from the game in 1974, Pelé signed a $4.75 million contract—the largest in sports history at the time—with the New York Cosmos of the North American Soccer League. He helped the game grow in America and when he retired on October 1, 1977, soccer lost its leading light.

Oscar Robertson

Oscar Robertson, here guarding the Boston Celtics' Sam Jones (above), was basketball's most well-rounded player.

 VERSATILITY IS A RARE COMMODITY at the highest levels of sports, where specialists abound. Today, the Los Angeles Lakers' Magic Johnson, a 6-foot-9 athlete who is equally adept at playing point guard as well as center, is seen as basketball's ultimate swing man. With all due respect, he is merely working toward a standard defined twenty years earlier by one Oscar Palmer Robertson.

"He is," says Hall of Fame guard Bob Cousy, "the greatest all-around player to come down the pike in my lifetime."

Bob Pettit, a Hall of Fame forward, adds, "Oscar gets my vote for the best all-around player ever."

Johnson has brought into vogue the so-called triple-double, a reference to a game in which the player averages double figures in points scored, rebounds, and assists. Well, for one amazing season, "Big O" averaged the elusive triple-double. In 1961–62, he averaged 30.8 points, 12.5 rebounds, and 11.4 assists for the Cincinnati Royals. That kind of across-the-board talent may never be seen again.

Robertson was born in Charlotte, Tennessee in 1938 and learned his craft in basketball-mad Indiana. He led his Crispus Attucks High School (Indianapolis) basketball team to the first undefeated season in the history of Indiana scholastic basketball. They had a string of forty-five consecutive wins and two state titles. In 1956, Robertson was named the Indiana Player of the Year as a senior. At the University of Cincinnati, Robertson's game flourished. "The only way to stop him," said Lou Rossini, the New York University coach, "is to put four men on him and have your fifth man guard the other Cincinnati players. Maybe even that won't work."

Robertson, by now a 6-foot-5 guard, did it all for the Bearcats, but functioned primarily as a scorer, averaging 33.9 points per game in his four seasons. His last collegiate seasons yielded averages of 35.1, 32.6, and 33.7 points per game, which were good for three

© UPI/Bettmann NewsPhotos

© UPI/Bettmann NewsPhotos

The Big O had an eye for the basket. In college, he averaged 33.9 points per game; in the pros, he concentrated on passing and defense as well.

national scoring titles and three consecutive College Player of the Year awards. Though Robertson set a new collegiate scoring mark that stood until Pete Maravich came along, Cincinnati failed to win the National Collegiate Athletic Association title, losing twice in the semifinals his last two years. This lack of team success dogged Robertson throughout his career and caused him great frustration.

Before he joined the Royals of the National Basketball Association, the team had twice placed last in its division with dismal, identical nineteen-win seasons. In his first three seasons, the Royals won thirty-three games, then progressed to forty-three in 1961. The athlete who led the United States to victory in the Pan-American Games and, later, the basketball gold medal in the 1960 Summer Olympic Games in Rome, Italy, made an instant impact. Robertson averaged 30.5 points per game, third in the entire league, behind Wilt Chamberlain and Elgin Baylor, and was named Rookie of the Year.

Robertson put together his unforgettable season in 1961–62 and by 1963 the Royals had become a respectable basketball team. "I don't like to talk about that season," Robertson said years later. "It makes me angry just to think about it. We had the best team in the NBA and we blew the championship." This is true. The Royals finished the regular-season four games behind the Boston Celtics in the Eastern Division, and eventually lost four of five games to the Celtics in the playoffs. That Robertson was the league's Most Valuable Player that season, with a 31.4-point and 11.0-assist average was somehow not the point to "Big O." He would ultimately win his first and only NBA title in 1971, when the aging veteran teamed with the young Kareem Abdul-Jabbar and the Milwaukee Bucks.

The legacy Robertson left is rich: In fourteen seasons, he scored 26,710 points and produced 9,887 assists and 7,804 rebounds. He was an All-Star the first twelve seasons of his career and averaged a record twenty points in those games.

© UPI/Bettmann NewsPhotos

Eddie Robinson

Eddie Robinson, the grand coach of Grambling, may be the most under-rated college football coach in history.

 ON THEIR FIRST POSSESSION THIS historic October 5, 1985 day, the Grambling Tigers moved seventy-seven yards for a touchdown. Quarterback Terrell Landry reached tight end Arthur Wells with a twelve-yard pass, and Grambling led Prairie View A&M 7–0 less than five minutes into the game. Grambling had not lost to Prairie View in eighteen previous meetings, but this one was something special. The lead would never be threatened and Coach Eddie Robinson was, at the age of sixty-six, finally, undeniably, the win-ningest college football coach ever. The 27–7 win at

the Cotton Bowl in Dallas, Texas, was the 324th of his forty-four-year career and pushed him one past University of Alabama Coach Paul "Bear" Bryant.

"It belongs to you, it belongs to the coaches, it belongs to Grambling," Robinson told his players in the locker room. "I'm just somebody out there trying to serve the youth. Anybody here in this room can do anything in the world he wants to do if he is willing to prepare himself. This is what we want to do; to be better men for having played the game. I just want to tell you that you are living in the best country in the world."

It might have sounded like a Hollywood script, but Robinson believed it, and so do the more than two hundred athletes he sent into the professional ranks over the years. The philosophy of life before football, a refreshing reversal of some major college programs, is the benchmark of Robinson's style, which ultimately helped America begin to accept black athletes.

Robinson, born on February 13, 1919, stepped into his first head-coaching job at the tender age of twenty-two. He was named to guide the football team at the Louisiana Negro Normal and Industrial Institute in Grambling, Louisiana. "We didn't have much to look forward to, but even less to look back on," Robinson said of the anonymous school and its unknown football program. His first victory came on November 15, 1941, when Grambling handed Tillotson College a 37–6 loss. Soon, Grambling was a power in college football. Robinson's teams, stocked with some of the country's best talent, rose to prominence and other schools began following his example and recruiting in places they had never looked. The school's fame spread as the victories mounted. Grambling, always forward-thinking, played the first regular-season collegiate football game in Japan in 1976.

As the 1980s approached, it became clear that Robinson was gaining on Alabama's celebrated Bryant. On September 25, 1982, Grambling defeated Florida A&M by a score of 43–21 to give Robinson his 300th win. Meanwhile, after the 1982 season, Bryant retired after twenty-five seasons at Alabama, plus a

year at the University of Maryland, eight at the University of Kentucky, and four at Texas A&M. His final record was 323–85–17. Robinson moved into second place on the all-time list on September 29, 1984, when Grambling's 42–0 rout of Prairie View ran his total to 315. That set the stage for his record-breaking victory the following year in Dallas. Grambling's impressive 8–3 record in 1988 moved Robinson's total to 349–122–15, a monstrous figure that is likely to stand for a long, long time. At the age of sixty-nine, Robinson showed no signs of retiring. The record, he maintained, was not as important as the teaching and molding of young men. "All it means is that I've been around a long time," he said. But, of course, it means much more than that.

In Super Bowl XXII, on January 31, 1988, Doug Williams of the Washington Redskins became living proof of Robinson's words. As the first starting black quarterback in Super Bowl history, Williams almost single-handedly destroyed the Denver Broncos, completing eighteen of twenty-nine passes for 340 yards and four touchdowns. At Grambling, Williams had directed the Tigers to a 35–5 record as a four-year starter. He was an All-American as a senior in 1977 and placed fourth in the Heisman Trophy balloting. At the urging of Robinson, Williams prepared himself for this important Super Bowl moment. After years of struggling professionally, Williams was named the game's Most Valuable Player, a fitting tribute to the philosophy of Eddie Robinson.

Robinson takes pride in the fact that he molds great men as well as great players.

Pete Rose

© Will Hart/AllSport

Though Pete Rose ultimately may be remembered best for his gambling, his ferocious spirit must not be forgotten.

HE IS THE GREAT AMERICAN SUCcess Story in the Great American Game. Like a typical youngster, Peter Edward Rose was fascinated with baseball while he was growing up in Cincinnati, Ohio. Yet, unlike anyone before, and possibly after, Rose mastered the art of hitting a baseball. It is considered the single most difficult feat in professional sports, but Rose's science of sweat and determination culminated in one of the game's most memorable moments on September 11, 1985.

Eric Show was on the mound for the San Diego Padres when the Reds' first baseman dug in at the plate in Cincinnati's Riverfront Stadium. With the count two and one, Show delivered a slider that Rose lashed into left field. At 8:01 p.m., the ball dropped in front of left fielder Carmelo Martinez, and Rose had secured the 4,192nd hit of his twenty-three-year career. Until that moment, Ty Cobb's hit record had stood for fifty-seven years. The 47,237 hometown fans rose in tribute, and, suddenly, the accomplishment began to sink in. "I didn't know what to do," Rose said later. "I've never been on a ball field and not known what to do." And then Rose, the relentless, hard-nosed man who had pursued Cobb for so long, broke down and cried. It had been fifteen years since tears had stained his face (when his father died), but there was Rose at the center of the deafening noise, shaking his head and blinking his eyes. "I'm not smart enough to have words to describe my feelings," Rose said. "I felt like a man looking for a hole to jump into. I looked around for someone to talk to and there wasn't anyone. I was doing all right until I looked up in the sky and saw my father, he was sitting in the front row, and Ty Cobb was sitting behind him. I'm tough, but I couldn't handle it. I didn't have anyone to talk to and some guy even took the base. I didn't have anything to kick."

Like Cobb, Rose was not universally loved by his peers, or the sporting public, for that matter. In 1989, he was banished from baseball for life. He was too aggressive, too driven. Rose, a 5-foot-11, 200-pound switch-hitter, ran to first base after receiving a walk, recklessly slid into second and third on his stomach, and chased down balls in the outfield with a zeal that never seemed to abate. After 1986, when he settled down into the manager's job at Cincinnati, Rose had set new career baseball standards for hits (4,256), games played (3,562), plate appearances (15,890), singles (3,215), and seasons with two hundred or more hits (10).

Born on April 14, 1941, in Cincinnati, Rose was obviously his father's child, for Harry Rose insisted on excellence. "Peter's father always stressed consistency," his mother, LaVerne, remembers. "When Peter was a boy, he would get four hits and come up to his father, obviously proud. I would be waiting in the car and want to cry. Each night before Peter would go to sleep, his dad would make him swing a bat nearly one hundred times, first from the right side, then from the left. His father is the reason he is such a great

Charlie Hustle ran to first base when others walked.

player. He just kept pushing him, but at the same time made playing sports fun. I know that is why Peter has maintained the enthusiasm all these years." He was two years old when his father, a banker, bought him his first glove, bat, and ball.

In 1960, the nineteen-year-old second baseman committed a league-high thirty-six errors in the New York-Pennsylvania League; however, a year later he led the Florida State League with 160 hits in 130 games, including thirty triples. After another year in the minors, Rose arrived at Reds' spring training camp in 1963. It was Mickey Mantle who first called Rose "Charlie Hustle," but by the end of the season most people in baseball knew that Rose's *modus operandi* was perpetual motion. He hit .273 that first season and was named Rookie of the Year. In a game dominated by home run hitters, Rose made hitting singles fashionable again. For nine straight seasons, from 1965 to 1973, Rose hit .300 or better.

Rose, a student of the game, is aware that he needed 2,300 more at-bats to reach Cobb's record of 4,192 hits. "I will never say I was a better baseball player than Cobb," he said. "All I'll say is I got more hits than he did. But I can say that when Cobb played, few people had heard about relief pitchers. The starters went the entire game most of the time. In my era, relief pitchers come in with fresh arms in the late innings. And the travel is fatiguing nowadays. In Cobb's day, the longest trip was a train from the East Coast to St. Louis. Now, we fly coast-to-coast, many times without a day off. The jet lag gets you sometimes because it's difficult to adjust to the time change. Still, Ty Cobb was a great player. I think I would have liked him."

And vice versa. After Rose set the record, Ronald Reagan, the President of the United States, talked with him by telephone in a conversation from home plate that was carried over the public address system. Rose, Reagan said, had set "the most enduring record in sports history."

Rose smiled and said, "Thank you, Mr. President, for taking time from your busy schedule." He paused and smiled again. "And you missed a good game."

Bill Russell

EVERY SPORT HAS ITS GIANTS, MEN and women who revolutionize their particular game with uncommon skill and technique. William F. Russell was that man in the stunning evolution of basketball. He defined the center position and its contemporary non-stop, both-ends-of-the-court role. Moreover, Russell helped push basketball into its place among the world's most popular sports. His rivalry with the great Wilt Chamberlain was one of the chief platforms in that swift elevation of the game.

"Basketball is like war, in that offensive weapons are developed first and it always takes awhile for the defense to catch up," said Boston Celtics Coach Red Auerbach, back in the 1960s. "Russell has had the biggest impact on the game of anyone in the last ten years because he instituted a new defense weapon, that of the blocked shot. He has popularized the weapon to combat the aggressive, running-type game. He is by far the greatest center ever to play the game." Of course, Auerbach could be accused of being slightly biased, since he coached Russell for so many years and later chose Russell personally as his successor. Still, in 1980 the Professional Basketball

His hook shot, when he took it, was consistent, but Bill Russell's gift to basketball was a dominant defensive presence.

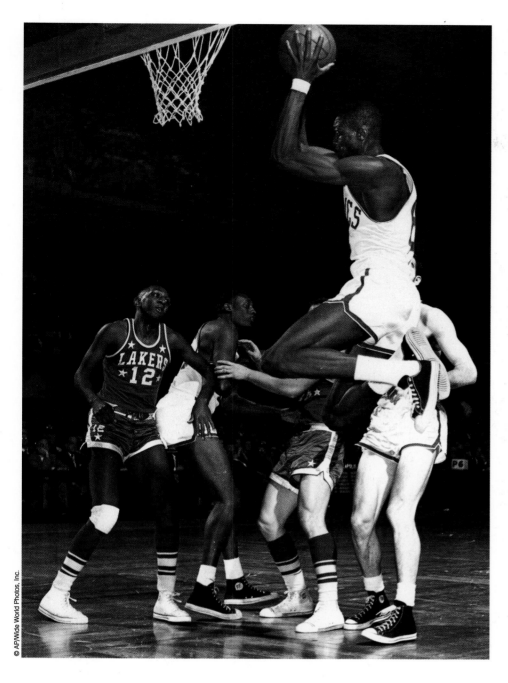

When Russell left the NBA after thirteen seasons, he left eleven championship banners behind.

Writers of America named Russell as The Greatest Player in the History of the National Basketball Association.

Russell was born in Monroe, Louisiana in 1934 and later grew up in a black ghetto in Oakland, California. Coming out of McClymonds High School, Russell stood 6-foot-5 and weighed 158 pounds. His defensive basketball abilities were a compensation for the offensive skills he lacked. He was a bench warmer his first three seasons and even as a starter on the Oakland Prep champions, he never scored more than fourteen points. Russell accepted a scholarship from the University of San Francisco and gradually began to fill out. Russell honed his defensive game, learning how to launch his gaunt body through the air so that he met the ball at its zenith. As he progressed, he discovered that a subtle touch could send the ball to a teammate, rather than out of bounds. This ignited the San Francisco fast break and, along with Russell's rebounding determination, would lead to a fifty-six-game winning streak for the Dons and two consecutive National Collegiate Athletic Association championships. Then Russell helped the United States Olympic basketball team win the gold medal in the 1956 Summer Games at Melbourne, Australia.

By the time he reached the Celtics, Russell stood 6-foot-10, weighed 220 pounds, and had begun to discover an offensive touch. Boston had never before won a league or division title, but with Russell playing an important role, they won the NBA crown, giving Russell three championships in a span of thirteen months. In thirteen seasons with the Celtics, Russell won eleven championship banners, including eight straight. The league's highest-paid rookie led the NBA in rebounding with 19.6 per game. The intimidation he lent to the low post position gave Celtics scorers like Bob Cousy and Bill Sharman more room to maneuver at the other end of the court.

In the Celtics' scheme of things, Russell was primarily a defensive player, although he managed to average fifteen points per game over his career, totalling 14,522 points. In that relatively brief career, Russell took down 21,721 rebounds, second on the all-time list behind Chamberlain. He was the league's Most Valuable Player five times, in 1958, 1961, 1962, 1963, and 1965, and an eleven-time All-Star. As Boston's player-coach for three seasons, Russell led the Celtics to two titles before retiring in 1969. He has appeared in various basketball roles, as broadcaster, coach, and general manager, and continues to be one of the most intelligent observers of the game.

Russell was cognizant of his role in the game and articulated his method with rare understanding. "Basketball is a game that involves a great deal of psychology," Russell said. "The psychology in defense is not blocking a shot or stealing a pass or getting the ball away. The psychology is to make the offensive team deviate from their normal habits. This is a game of habits, and the player with the most consistent habits is the best. What I try to do on defense is to make the offensive man do not what he wants, but what I want. I might block only five shots in a game, but I'm the only one who knows which five."

The Babe was larger than legend. To this day, no one hit the ball harder, or more often, than George Herman Ruth.

 OF ALL THE FAMOUS ATHLETES across the history of sporting experience, the word legend seems most appropriate when referring to George Herman Ruth.

More often, he was simply called "Babe," or the "Bambino," or the magnificent "Sultan of Swat." All the labels fell short of the man himself; Babe Ruth strode across baseball and, ultimately, the entire United States during the golden age of sports, the roaring 1920s. Until the time of Hank Aaron, the legend that Ruth built seemed unapproachable; he hit 714 home runs and knocked in 2,211 runs in twenty-two seasons. The record book shows that Ruth is second to Aaron in both these categories, but he remains the all-time leader in slugging percentage (.690) and bases on balls (2,056). Ruth is baseball's quintessential slugger, however, because he hit home runs more often than any other man. He averaged one home run for every 11.76 at-bats, compared to Aaron who failed to even reach the all-time top ten, with a figure of 16.38.

He was born on February 6, 1895 and, at least early on, lived a turbulent life in Baltimore, Maryland. Ruth was placed in St. Mary's Industrial Home for Boys, a reform school for young men thought to be beyond hope. His mother died when he was fifteen, and eight years later his father was killed in a brawl outside the bar he owned. Jack Dunn, the president of the Orioles of the International League signed the left-handed pitcher and catcher to a contract fresh out of high school. When Ruth was nineteen, Dunn's Ori-

oles went bankrupt and he sold Ruth's rights to the Boston Red Sox for the huge sum of $2,900. Though the Boston Red Sox returned the hurler briefly to the minors in Baltimore and Providence, Rhode Island, he was recalled later the same summer with a record of 22–9. Never again were his talents questioned.

Ruth wasn't much of a hitter his first three seasons and was viewed primarily as a pitcher. That first fractured season in the majors produced exactly two hits in ten at-bats in a pinch-hitting role. The next two years he only reached the plate 228 times and managed sixty-three hits. At 6-foot-2, 215 pounds, Ruth was a phenomenal athlete. And though later he gained weight and appeared sluggish in the outfield, he was more than adequate defensively and fairly nimble on the bases in his early years. In his first full season, 1915, Ruth led all American League pitchers with eighteen victories. As the Red Sox won three World Series in four years, Ruth's ability as a hitter continued to emerge. When Boston's wave of dominance ended with a six-game victory over Chicago in the 1918 World Series, Ruth had already begun the transition to full-time hitter. He won two games on the mound, but the Red Sox finally realized he was more valuable in the lineup every day.

In 1919, Ruth made 432 plate appearances and led the American League in home runs (twenty-nine), runs (103), runs batted in (114), and slugging percent-age (.657). Though Ruth was 9–5 on the mound that season, the secret was out. The New York Yankees liked what they saw, and when Boston owner Harry Frazee found himself financially strapped, they made him an offer he couldn't refuse. In return for $125,000 in cash and a $300,000 loan, New York received Ruth for what would turn out to be sixteen glorious years. Ruth won all five of the games he pitched over that period to run his career record to 94–46, but his bat was the main attraction.

Ruth's first two seasons in New York were, well, Ruthian in proportion. In 1920, he hit fifty-four homers, scored 158 runs, knocked in 137 runs, and slugged .847, the highest one-season average ever. Ruth also walked 148 times, a tribute to his discerning eye at the plate. A year later, he hit fifty-nine homers, scored a staggering 177 runs, and knocked in another 171. When his career ended after the 1932 season, Ruth had hoisted numbers that only Aaron would reach.

When somebody rises to the top of his particular field, the name of Babe Ruth invariably emerges by way of comparison. As Robert W. Creamer points out in his terrific biography, "...forty years after his last game...almost every day, certainly several times a week, you read and hear about him." To be the "Babe Ruth" of any discipline is the goal. As long as the memories of Ruth and his crisp, majestic blows over the outfield fence linger, all comparisons will fall short.

Old timers say that if Ruth had remained a pitcher, he would have made the Hall of Fame that way, too.

Willie Shoemaker

In forty years of horse racing, Shoemaker produced some staggering numbers, including nearly 9,000 winners. Shoemaker's triumph in the 1986 Kentucky Derby (above) was the perfectly surprising climax to a celebrated career.

 THE FIFTY-FOUR-YEAR-OLD JOCKEY sat at home in San Marino, California with his wife and watched Jack Nicklaus, at forty-six, win the 1986 Masters. "This is an omen," Shoemaker told his wife Cindy. "They thought he was washed up, finished, and he just won the Masters. If Nicklaus can win the Masters, I can win the Kentucky Derby."

In one of the most enchanting rides in the history of thoroughbred racing, Shoemaker won the 1986 Kentucky Derby aboard Ferdinand, a seventeen-to-one shot. It had been twenty-one years since his last Derby triumph, when Lucky Debonair took him to the third and seemingly final crown at Churchill Downs. At an age when most jockies have long since retired, "The Shoe" was still standing tall in the saddle, although many critics suggested he was past his prime. Not so. "John Longden rode until he was fifty-nine and did damn well," said Shoemaker's trainer, seventy-three-year-old Charles Whittingham. "Bill's never had to worry about his weight, like other riders. You go play golf with him some day, and he'll make you throw away your clubs."

Shoemaker's win took everyone back to the 1950s and 1960s, when he was the world's dominant jockey, blessed as he was with sweet hands of gentle power. In the 1986 Derby, Shoemaker and Ferdinand trailed the entire field early, then steadily picked their way

through horse after horse. At the top of the home-stretch, Shoemaker found a hole in traffic and moved his horse along the rail. Ferdinand beat Bold Arrangement and Broad Brush to the wire in a time of 2 minutes, 2.45 seconds for the mile and one-quarter track. "What a feeling," Shoemaker exclaimed as he stepped down in the victory circle. "I was half in shock. It's just a great feeling to be able to do that at this stage of my life, you know?"

The victory was a perfect punctuation mark on the career of the world's greatest jockey, for through 1988 Shoemaker had produced some potentially unreachable numbers: In forty years of brilliant racing, Shoemaker saddled up 40,056 times, won a record 8,788 times, placed on 6,094 occasions, and shown 4,953 other times. The prize money amounted to a staggering $121,753,000, the standard 10 percent commission for his mounts' winnings.

William Lee Shoemaker was born on August 19, 1931 in Fabens, Texas. While it makes a nice story, Shoemaker never rode a horse while living in Texas. At the age of ten, he moved to El Monte, California and five years later began working at the Suzy Q Ranch in Puente. Shoemaker had established himself as an unbeaten boxer and wrestler in high school, but his short stature forced him out of the dating scene and into tending horses. By the age of sixteen, Shoemaker decided on a career in racing. After exercising horses at the Santa Anita racetrack, trainer George Reeves allowed him to explore his potential as a jockey. His first victory came on April 20, 1949. "It was at Golden Gate and my third race," Shoemaker says. "I was up on Shafter V. He was nine to one but he should have been four to five. He won like that anyway." Shoemaker rode 219 winners that year, a record surpassed at the time by only Gordon Glisson's 270. His purses that year totalled $458,010 and Shoemaker, by then 4-foot-11, ninety-eight pounds, was on his way.

In his second full year, Shoemaker and Joe Culmone made national headlines as they battled for top jockey honors. They finished with 388 winners each and the next year, 1951, Shoemaker emerged as the leading winner with $1.329 million in purses. In October 1953, Shoemaker set a world record for victories in a calendar year, with his 392nd at Golden Gate; he finished the year with 485. Shoemaker won the 1955 Kentucky Derby aboard Swaps, but two years later made a classic error by sitting up in the saddle too quickly, allowing Iron Liege to slip past and ruin a certain victory for Gallant Man. In 1959, Shoemaker rebounded with a Kentucky Derby win on Tommy Lee. In 1965, after leading all jockeys in winnings for seven consecutive years, Shoemaker was edged by Braulio Baeza.

Shoemaker's trademark is his supreme confidence; people in the thoroughbred game say his greatness comes in transmitting that belief to his mount. "The big thing is to relax," he says. "Lots of jocks are tense. Somehow I think my relaxation gets across to the horse, makes him want to run. I ride with a longer hold because that way I get a horse in hand, running against the bit. I can feel him and he can feel me. I think a long hold enables both horse and rider to relax more."

O.J. Simpson

THE GRAY SKY OVER SHEA STADIUM on December 16, 1973 did not bode particularly well for Orenthal James Simpson. There was snow on the frozen field, and running backs in professional football traditionally like to keep their feet (not to mention their wits) about them. Still, it had been a sensational season for the Buffalo Bills halfback and his offensive line, the "Electric Company," so named because they turned on the "Juice." O.J. Simpson had opened the season with a 250-yard effort against the New England Patriots, and heading into this regular-season finale against the New York Jets, Simpson had gained 1,803 yards, sixty-one short of Jim Brown's National Football League single-season rushing record. Could Simpson run into history on this dreary day?

Silly question. Simpson gained fifty-seven yards on the Bills' opening drive and on Buffalo's second possession, Simpson bolted through a hole created by left guard Reggie McKenzie and fullback James Braxton. The six-yard run broke Brown's record.

"Was the hole big enough?" Braxton wondered.

"Looked okay to me," Simpson replied. "Let's get some more."

And so it was that Simpson finished the day with 200 yards on thirty-four carries. That pushed his 1973 total to an unbelievable 2,003 yards. And though Eric Dickerson, playing for the Los Angeles Rams, gained 2,105 yards in 1984, Simpson's fourteen-game achievement was a milestone in sports. Consider that when Dickerson broke Simpson's record it was in the fifteenth game of a sixteen-game schedule and he averaged a half yard less in doing it. "When I was thirteen or fourteen I once ran into Jimmy Brown in a

On this gray day in New York, Simpson's achievement was frozen in time. He became the first man to surpass 2,000 yards rushing in a single season.

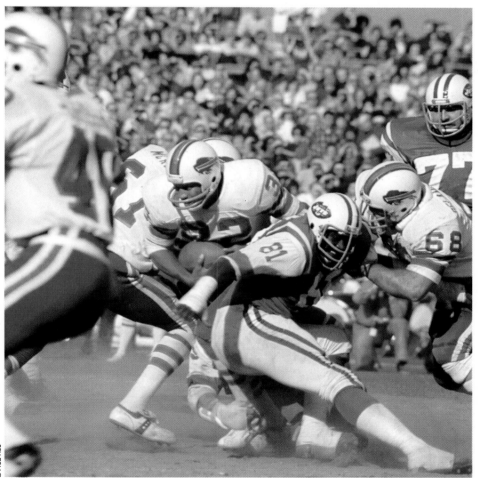

Even playing for the Buffalo Bills, Simpson was able to churn out impressive yardage with a variety of breathtaking moves.

cago Bears. He gained 11,236 yards, scored seventy touchdowns, and caught 203 passes. And Simpson did it with speed, style, and elegance. He had the speed of a world-class sprinter and the uncommon ability to see holes a fraction of a second before they opened up. Simpson's acceleration and ability to change direction at will made him a very difficult target, indeed.

Simpson's greatness is underlined by the fact that he played for a poor team. The Bills won only one game in 1968, thereby winning the right to draft the University of Southern California tailback who had won the Heisman Trophy. Simpson's college exploits filled two or three highlight films, but Buffalo wasn't used to these kind of pyrotechnics. The Bills lost thirty-three of forty-two games during Simpson's first three seasons, when he operated without the aid of any visible blocking. Eventually, the Bills' brain trust began to build an offensive line around its greatest asset. In 1972, Simpson broke through and led the NFL in rushing with 1,251 yards, the first of five consecutive seasons over 1,000 yards, something only Franco Harris, Walter Payton, and Eric Dickerson ever improved upon. A year later, he cracked the 2,000-yard barrier.

Though Simpson endured a series of injuries over the years, when he was healthy he got stronger as the game grew longer. This explains his record of six games of two hundred yards or more.

In 1985, when Simpson was enshrined in the Hall of Fame with a star-studded class that included quarterbacks Joe Namath and Roger Staubach, he technically became the first Heisman Trophy winner to reach that sacred professional ground; based on alphabetical order, he nudged fellow Heisman-winner Staubach. Simpson was the first man to make the difficult transition from college to the professional ranks without missing so much as a step.

candy store," Simpson said after the game. "I told him I was going to break his record, like a kid will do. Now that I've done it, it's a little hard to believe." Three days later, Simpson's number thirty-two uniform, in all its bloody, muddy splendor was hanging in the Pro Football Hall of Fame in Canton, Ohio.

Brown, of course, is the standard against which football running backs are measured. Simpson isn't terribly far behind. From 1969–78, Simpson was the bridge between Brown and Walter Payton of the Chi-

Mark Spitz

MARK SPITZ NEVER WON ANY MEDALS for humility. After triumphing in the 1967 Pan-American Games, the eighteen-year-old predicted he would win six gold medals in Mexico City, site of the 1968 Summer Olympic Games. The self-inflicted pressure proved to be too much and he finished with only two golds, both relay medals. Spitz placed second in the 100-meter butterfly, third in the 100-meter freestyle, and a distant eighth in his specialty, the 200-meter butterfly, eight seconds slower than his world record. Some of his teammates on the United States swim team were thrilled. Don Schollander, who won four golds in 1964 in Tokyo, Japan, was only one of them.

Competitors claimed he was spoiled; certainly, Spitz had a fairly typical champion's upbringing. His successful father pushed hard, while his mother sacrificed and drove him to 5 a.m. practice sessions. Ultimately, the family moved to give Spitz, born on February 10, 1950 in Modesto, California, access to a better training program at the Arden Hills Club. Success came early and often, and by the time he reached Mexico City, Spitz could be forgiven for thinking he couldn't fail. His coach at Arden Hills, Sherman Chavoor, suggested that anti-Semitism, even from fellow members of the U.S. swimming team, worked against Spitz in 1968, but it was more likely attributed to his nervous disposition.

Shattered, Spitz decided to enroll at Indiana University as a pre-dental student. There, under the guidance of coach Doc Counsilman, Spitz matured and learned the nature of teamwork. The Hoosiers won three straight National Collegiate Athletic Association titles with Spitz leading the way. He graduated in 1972, and as the Munich, West Germany Olympic Games approached, Spitz wasn't making any public predictions. No matter, for others felt he could eclipse Schollander's record by winning seven gold medals. This had never happened before in a single Olympiad; Italian fencer Nedo Nadi held the record of five, set in Antwerp, Belgium in 1920.

As Spitz stepped onto the block for the first of his seven races in Munich on August 28, 1972, he was noticeably ill-at-ease. Swimmers are generally less than calm as they face the pool for a start, but as Spitz contemplated the 200-meter butterfly before him, he was undoubtedly flooded with bad memories of his spectacular failure in Mexico City. This time, however, Spitz produced the race of his life. He won by more than two seconds, a huge margin in swimming, and broke his own world record with a time of two minutes 00.7 seconds. That set the stage for the greatest sustained Olympic performance in history.

Later that day came the 4 x 100-meter relay, which the United States won in three minutes, 26.42 seconds. Spitz won his third gold the next day with a commanding victory in the 200-meter freestyle, racing to a time of 1 minute, 52.78 seconds, another world record. Two more records fell when Spitz won the 100-meter butterfly (54.27 seconds) and participated in the winning of 4 x 200-meter freestyle team that was timed in seven minutes, 35.78 seconds. At this point, Spitz had five gold medals and was fairly assured of another, in the 4 x 100 medley relay. He was entered

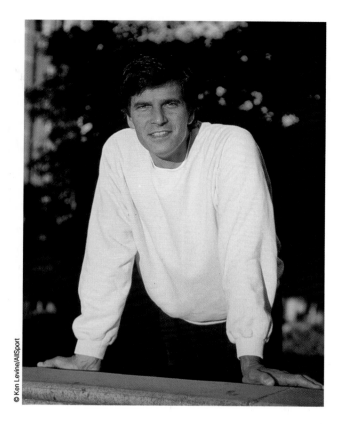

in the 100-meter freestyle, but considered pulling out because U.S. teammate Jerry Heidenreich was swimming well. Chavoor intervened and told Spitz in no uncertain terms that history would view him unkindly if he ducked the challenge. Spitz relented and narrowly defeated Heidenreich with a world-record time of 51.22. The 4 x 100 medley relay went as planned and the U.S. team cruised to a 3:48.16 win.

When it was all over, Spitz had turned the swimming world upside down over an eight-day span: seven races, seven gold medals, seven world records. No one ever did it better than Mark Spitz in the Munich Summer Olympic Games.

Unbelievably, the vintage butterfly form that reaped gold in Munich is likely to be on back-to-the-future display in the 1992 Summer Olympics. Spitz swam seven times in Munich and won seven gold medals, a record that may never be broken.

Jim Thorpe

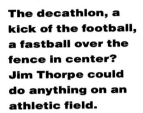

The decathlon, a kick of the football, a fastball over the fence in center? Jim Thorpe could do anything on an athletic field.

 JAMES FRANCIS THORPE HAD JUST won the decathlon and pentathlon events at the 1912 Summer Olympic Games in Stockholm, Sweden. After the Native American had won four of the pentathlon's five events and four of the trying decathlon's ten disciplines, King Gustav, a learned sports fan, presented Thorpe with his second gold medal of the competition. "Sir," the King said with admiration, "you are the greatest athlete in the world." The point is still debatable.

Thorpe was born in a one-room cabin near Prague, Oklahoma, on May 28, 1888, along with a twin brother who died at an early age. His mother was three-fourths Indian and his father was one-half. Among the Sac and Fox Indians, Thorpe was known as Wa-tho-huk, or Bright Path. At the age of sixteen, Thorpe was recruited by the United States Indian Industrial School in Carlisle, Pennsylvania, commonly called the Carlisle Institute. Thorpe chose to become a tailor, but two years later he competed in organized sports for the first time. He was a guard on the tailors' football team in the Shop league. Soon, Carlisle was playing a major college schedule under the direction of coach Glenn "Pop" Warner. "The entire student body comprised no more than two hundred and fifty boys," Warner said many years later. "They were all youngsters—including Thorpe. They were really high school boys playing against men . . . but my God, how they could play!"

The 6-foot-1, 180-pound Thorpe had everything: laser-sharp reflexes, speed, power, and desire. The All-American led Carlisle to an upset of highly regarded Harvard University to finish the 1911 season on a high note. Thorpe, a marvelous runner and kicker, scored all of his team's points with one touchdown and four field goals. The next season, "The Nomads of the Gridiron" traveled the country and met some of the best teams. Thorpe scored twenty-five touchdowns in 1912 and totaled 198 points. He scored twenty-eight of Carlisle's thirty-four points against Pittsburgh and twenty-two in a 27-6 victory over Army. The key play in the Army game was a fake punt, followed by a ninety-yard touchdown run.

In addition to football, Thorpe was Carlisle's best in virtually every sport. He was a hard-hitting first baseman; an unbeaten hurdler, jumper, and sprinter; peerless in basketball, lacrosse, and wrestling. When Pop Warner arrived in Easton, Pennsylvania with his one-man track team, Lafayette's track coach wanted to know where the rest of the Carlisle track team was. "Here it is," said Warner, pointing to Thorpe. Needless to say, Thorpe routed Lafayette, winning nearly every event.

The Stockholm Olympics had already come and gone when the Amateur Athletic Union declared that Thorpe was no longer an amateur because he had accepted money for playing baseball with the Rocky Mount team in North Carolina. Indeed, after school let out, Thorpe had joined two former Carlisle teammates in the summer months of 1909. "I got short of money," Thorpe said, "so when the manager offered me fifteen dollars a week to play third base, I didn't even think about doing anything wrong, because there were a lot of other college boys playing there." It wasn't long before the International Olympic Committee stripped Thorpe of his medals.

He played major league baseball for seven summers, from 1913 to 1919, but Thorpe's greatest mark was made on the football field, though he didn't start playing professionally until he was thirty-two. By that time, he was running on battered legs and his concentration and dedication, never the best, lapsed frequently, along with a resistance to distilled spirits of various kinds. Still, Thorpe was the heart of the Canton Bulldogs for three years before tours with the Cleveland Indians and Rock Island, a now defunct franchise. Thorpe played one last season for Canton before retiring. He died in poverty after working a series of jobs that ranged from digging ditches to handling security in an automobile plant. To the end, he longed for his gold medals.

"I'd be the happiest man in the world if I could get my medals back," he said before he died. "At least they couldn't strip me of the King's words. I played a little summer baseball while I was at Carlisle, for eating money. But whatever the competition, I played with the heart of an amateur—for the pure hell of it." Seventy years after its original decision and thirty years after Thorpe's death, the International Olympic Committee voted to restore his medals.

At 6-foot-1, 180 pounds, Thorpe basically carried the Carlisle team in 1911.

If early returns mean anything, Mike Tyson is destined to become the greatest heavyweight of all time.

Mike Tyson

MIKE TYSON, THE YOUNGEST HEAVYweight boxing champion in history, entered the most important bout of his young career on June 27, 1988 amid controversy and turmoil. In the opposite corner of the ring stood Michael Spinks, the thirty-one-year-old challenger with a spotless 31-0 record. Tyson, ten years younger, had defeated all of his previous thirty-four opponents. Still, people wondered if Tyson could overcome the distractions that had visited him since he knocked out Larry Holmes five months earlier. Tyson had married television star, Robin Givens, seen close friend and co-manager Jim Jacobs die a month later, then stood by as surviving manager Bill Cayton battled Tyson for control of his finances. The attendant swirl of publicity that sometimes comes with being heavyweight champion of the world threatened to box Tyson in as the richest prizefight in history began.

The first punch after the opening bell at Atlantic City, New Jersey was a left hook by Tyson that caught Spinks high on the head. "I noticed the fear come into his eyes then," Tyson would say later. Seconds later, Tyson's left uppercut snapped Spinks' head back. A short, right hook to the chest followed and Spinks fell to one knee for the first knockdown of his professional career. After a mandatory eight-count, Tyson's powerful right hand crashed against Spinks' jaw and the challenger was down; his head was still resting against the bottom rope when the referee finished counting him out. Tyson won by knockout in ninety-one seconds, four seconds fewer than singer Jeffrey Osborne required to render the pre-fight national anthem. It was the fourth-fastest heavyweight title fight in history and it established Tyson as one of history's greatest boxers.

"No matter what happens in my life, I'm a professional," Tyson said later, after earning approximately twenty million dollars for his brief trouble. "I took it right to him. It was either do or die. That's what I came out to do."

Tyson was raised, under difficult circumstances, to be a champion. He grew up knocking around New York City; he was arrested thirty-eight times as a youth for a variety of crimes, some of them violent. As he raged at his tattered environment, Tyson developed the anger that would carry him higher and faster than any heavyweight boxer ever. Cus D'Amato found the thirteen-year-old Tyson sparring in a reform school. D'Amato immediately recognized his talent and said, "You can be the champion of the world. You've got the size and speed to do it. If you listen to me and work real hard, I promise it will happen." And Tyson remembers wondering, "What is this crazy ol' white dude saying to me?"

Now, D'Amato was no ordinary boxing trainer; he had guided Floyd Patterson to the heavyweight title at the tender age of twenty-one years, eleven months. As the 6-foot, 221-pound Tyson became more polished in the ring, his reputation grew beyond upstate New York, where he knocked opponents out as quickly as they were lined up.

When Tyson stood on the threshold of the heavyweight title, he had won each of his twenty-eight fights, twenty-six by knockout. The raw, thickly muscled Tyson was a throwback; not only did he worship the ring legends of the past by taping their pictures on his wall, but he wore black trunks, no socks, and took fights every few months. By the time he faced Trevor Berbick on November 22, 1986, Tyson was into the twenty-first month of his professional career. He knocked Berbick down twice in the second round and, at two minutes and thirty-five seconds, the referee stopped the fight. The new champion of the world was aged twenty years, four months, and twenty-two days. D'Amato, who became Tyson's legal guardian in 1981, wasn't there to see it happen, however, having passed away a year earlier, but Tyson said, "I'm sure he was up there watching. This fight was for him."

Nine months later, Tyson produced another memorable feat, unifying the heavyweight title for the first time in ten years. In an unprecedented tournament, Tyson won the championship belts of the World Boxing Council, World Boxing Association, and International Boxing Federation in a span of sixteen months.

After a tumultuous layoff of eight months in which Tyson was divorced, lost his manager, and fired his trainer, he dispatched challenger Frank Bruno in the fifth round. Tyson's record stood at 36-0, including thirty-two knockouts. Ring experts were not only calling him the youngest heavyweight champion of all time, but one of the best.

Bonecrusher Smith was the bone-crushee in this 1987 bout with Tyson (below).

Johnny Unitas

© Manny Rubio

When people wonder if the San Francisco 49ers' Joe Montana is the greatest quarterback in NFL history, their comparisons inevitably invoke the name of Johnny Unitas.

 THE STREAK BEGAN INNOCENTLY enough in 1956, when the Baltimore Colts were something less than a power in the National Football League. Quarterback Johnny Unitas had begun his career inauspiciously with an interception, into the hands of Chicago's J.C. Caroline, who returned it for a touchdown. By season's end, Unitas had set a new record for completion percentage (55.6) by a rookie. In between, Unitas began a streak of forty-seven consecutive games with at least one touchdown pass, a standard of relentless brilliance that may never be equaled. In truth, it was a forty-nine-game streak, but the 1958 and 1959 championships generally aren't included into the equation. Still, Unitas' record included parts of five seasons, and some people believe it rivals Joe DiMaggio's fifty-six game hitting streak.

Comparisons between athletes of different eras are difficult because as the game evolves, habits and tactics change the boundaries of competition. So it was with Johnny Unitas, arguably the game's greatest quarterback. When he retired in 1973, Unitas held the NFL records for passes attempted (5,186), passes completed (2,830), passing yards (40,239), most seasons with 3,000 yards passing (3), most 300-yard games (twenty-six), and most touchdown passes (290). Fran Tarkenton and Dan Fouts eventually passed Unitas in attempts, completions, and yards, while Tarkenton threw up 342 touchdown passes, and Fouts produced fifty-one 300-yard-games. Though Tarkenton came along only five years later than Unitas, he played at a time when the passing game came out of the closet. He was generally the focal point of the offense and never played for a champion-

© AP/Wide World Photos, Inc.

© Manny Rubio

his best when the clock was running down and he had to move his team quickly down the field. He was a leader under pressure, as evidenced by the Colts' league championships in 1958 and 1959, and in 1971's Super Bowl V. Unitas set playoff records for highest completion percentage (62.9) and passing yards in championship play (1,177). On three different occasions, Unitas was the NFL's Most Valuable Player and also the MVP in three of the ten Pro Bowls he played in.

And to think that he almost didn't come to pass. That's right, Unitas almost slipped between the cracks in 1955. Not many of the NFL's teams were interested in the University of Louisville quarterback. The Pittsburgh Steelers drafted him in the ninth round, almost as an afterthought, and waived him before he had a chance to throw a single pass under game circumstances. Though Unitas was shattered, he signed with a Pittsburgh-area semi-professional team known as the Bloomfield Rams. He made six dollars a game and played before sparse crowds on shabby fields along the East Coast. Unitas' career might have ended there if not for a Bloomfield fan who sang praises to Unitas in a letter to Baltimore Colts Coach Weeb Ewbank. The Colts, seeing something the Steelers did not, signed Unitas to a $7,000 contract the following summer.

In the fourth game of the 1956 season, first string Colt quarterback George Shaw was lost to an injury, and the rookie came in and promptly threw an interception against the Bears. Nevertheless, Unitas led the Colts to a 4-4 record the rest of the season and became the established signal-caller. He threw twenty-four touchdown passes the following year and a career-high thirty-two in 1959. At the age of thirty-six, Unitas took the Colts to the Super Bowl and a 16-13 victory over the Dallas Cowboys.

For forty-seven consecutive games, an eternity in terms of the NFL, Johnny Unitas threw at least one touchdown pass per game.

ship team. Fouts, the mad bomber of San Diego, was never surrounded by the kind of talented players with whom Unitas shared the offensive wealth.

Unitas, 6-foot-1, 196 pounds, was not blessed with a magnificent arm or exceptional speed. What he had though, was football intelligence. He could see the whole field and more importantly, understood where to throw the football and when. Subtlety was Unitas' game; he was a master of the complex angles of the screen pass and always seemed to keep defenses off balance by calling the unexpected play. Unitas was at

Ted Williams

The 'splendid splinter' was the last man in the Major Leagues to maintain a .400 batting average through a season.

IN 1941, WHEN JOE DiMAGGIO WAS dominating the headlines as he put together his elegant fifty-six game hitting streak, Theodore Samuel Williams was out-hitting DiMaggio .412 to .408. Beyond that, Williams forged an unforgettable season as he became the last baseball player to hit .400 for the course of an entire season. And it was the way he did it that made the achievement so memorable. "I wanted to be the greatest hitter who ever lived," he wrote in his autobiography, *My Turn at Bat*. "It was the center of my heart, hitting a baseball."

Williams was born on August 30, 1918 in San Diego, California and twenty years later, when he first arrived in Boston, Williams was a scrawny 6-foot-3, 160 pounds. The rookie proceeded to set the American League on fire. He led all batters with 145 runs batted in, the best total ever by a rookie; hit .327; placed second in doubles (forty-four); and third in home runs (thirty-one). His 107 bases on balls, another rookie record, indicated his keen eye was already comfortable at the major league level.

The Boston Red Sox were playing the Philadelphia Athletics in a double-header to end the season and their slugger entered the game with a .39955 batting average. Williams turned on Philadelphia pitching for

three singles and his thirty-seventh home run of the year. Safely over the celebrated .400 mark, Williams could have watched the second game from the bench, as some players do today after reaching the .300 plateau. But no, Williams insisted on playing and managed a single and a double in the second game and finished the day six-for-eight with a season's average of .4057 (.406). Nevertheless, DiMaggio was voted the league's Most Valuable Player in 1941, over the man who had won it the year before.

Williams was never fully appreciated by the press who voted for the award, or by the fans for that matter. He believed that his on-field contribution was what mattered, not the care and feeding of writers' egos. Consequently, he was routinely and unfairly overlooked when it came to post-season honors. Nonetheless, Williams stands today as one of baseball's finest hitters. Never has anyone so thoroughly understood the strike zone. If he took a pitch, no matter how close, umpires invariably called it a ball.

"I could stare down every hitter who ever came up there," said Vic Raschi, the Yankees' gifted right-

Williams was among the handful of players to hit consistently for average and power. His slugging average of .634 is second on the all time list.

hander. "Except one. That's right, Ted Williams. Well, what do you do with a guy that's been staring at you from the moment he's left the dugout to go out onto the on-deck circle, and keeps his eyes on you when he's in the batter's box? Ted's concentration at the plate was so intense, I don't think he even knew what I was trying to do."

Rather, Williams was completely absorbed in what he, the hitter, was doing. Some people would argue that Williams followed through on his childhood dream and became the greatest hitter in baseball history. Though Williams' lifetime batting average of .344 was twenty-three points lower than Ty Cobb's, his power statistics (521 home runs and a .634 slugging percentage) were far superior. At the same time, Williams was a more consistent hitter than Babe Ruth, though his career numbers suffered because of interruptions by his military service. He missed three years in World War II, while in his middle twenties, then was recalled to active military duty during the Korean War and missed most of two more seasons.

He was an All-Star game hero in 1941 after a dramatic three-run homer off Claude Passeau with two out in the ninth. His .406 average that year gave him the first of six batting titles, to go with four home run championships, plus two triple crowns, in 1942 and 1947. Williams, ever the complete player, led the American League in slugging percentage nine different times, and once led the league in bases on balls, averaging 149 during one six-year stretch.

Williams maintained his skills far beyond the usual boundaries. In 1957, at the age of thirty-nine, he batted .388 to lead the league and hit thirty-eight home runs. The next year, his .328 average was again the standard. In 1960, his final season, Williams hit twenty-nine home runs. When he came to the plate in his last game, at the age of forty-two, Williams punctuated his career with one last blast out of the park.

John Wooden

The man with the rolled-up program guided the UCLA basketball team to a staggering ten national championship titles.

THOUGH THERE WERE FIVE MEN who coached men's Division I basketball teams to more victories over the years (Adolph Rupp, Phog Allen, Henry Iba, Ed Diddle, and Ray Meyer), John Robert Wooden brought a quality to his work that was unparalleled. "There is no easy explanation," he said at the height of his glory. "What we do is simple: get in condition, learn fundamentals, and play together. I don't buy the proposition that UCLA has risen above the general level of college basketball. We've been more consistent, come closer to our natural ability, more often than others. We've had a great run, and each season I can see this certain carryover to the new players. Subconsciously, they are almost afraid to fail. This encourages them to give more in practice and accept some things in the way of discipline that they wouldn't otherwise. I get away with methods other coaches have

trouble defining to their players, but I have no delusions. It's not me; it is because UCLA wins that the players don't give me more guff."

He was too modest, of course, for Wooden was the primary reason the University of California at Los Angeles was the dominant team in college basketball in the 1960s and 1970s. From 1964 to 1975, UCLA won ten National Collegiate Athletic Association basketball championships, an achievement of consistent excellence that was approached only by the University of Houston golf teams of the 1960s and the Oklahoma State University wrestling teams of the 1930s. Wooden and his Bruins established a series of records that may never be approached: eighty-eight consecutive victories (surpassing the old mark of sixty), ten NCAA titles (the previous best was four), an amazing seven consecutive crowns (surpassing the old record of two), thirty-eight straight NCAA tournament victories, and eight undefeated conference championships. In 1975, after winning that tenth title in twelve years, Wooden retired from coaching with an overall record of 905-203, an .820 winning percentage. A total of 667 victories came in the college ranks, the sixth-best figure of all time, though Wooden did not linger in the game as long as some of his peers.

Wooden's first success came on the basketball court, not alongside it. He was born in Martinsville, Indiana on October 14, 1910, and became a three-time All-State player at Martinsville High School. It was the same thing at Purdue University; Wooden was a three-time Helms All-America and captained the Boilermakers his last two seasons. If Wooden had never again been involved with basketball, his 1932 season might have carried him forever. As a senior, Wooden set a Big Ten scoring record, led Purdue to a national championship, and won College Player of the Year honors. After a professional stint with the Kautsky Grocers of Indianapolis, where he once sank 138 consecutive free throws, Wooden moved on to his true calling.

He coached Dayton High School in Kentucky for two years, then compiled a 218-42 record in nine years at Central High School in South Bend, Indiana. On his return from World War II, Wooden broke into the college ranks and prodded Indiana State Teachers' College to a two-year record of 47-14. In 1948, word of Wooden's uncommon talent reached the University of Minnesota and UCLA. While the phone lines in the upper midwest were down, Wooden accepted the job in Los Angeles. Minnesota got through one hour later, but it was too late; Wooden was heading for California. He inherited a team that returned no starters and a 12-13 record. Wooden found himself wondering why he took the job. "I was the most discouraged person so far as basketball was concerned," he said. "It really looked bad." Somehow, the Bruins won six straight games to open the season and, at one point, put together a twelve-game winning streak on the way to a 22-7 record. A stream of

talented players, including giants of the game like Lew Alcindor and Bill Walton, passed through his nurturing hands and UCLA became a powerhouse. Wooden's accomplishment of consistency is more remarkable than most of the professional dynasties, since the four-year college turnover is so rapid.

"As I look back," he said in 1972, "most everything I have is a result of sport. Oh, I know it's the toy part of the world and I'm not significant in any wordly fashion. But a long time ago I found this niche, and it has been right for me. I've enjoyed coaching, teaching, and the relationships. It's nice to look around and see my players become successful in different fields. I am content. I have peace of mind, and I worry about how much I'm going to miss this sport when I get out of it in the near future." Later that year, twelve seasons after he had been enshrined in the Basketball Hall of Fame in Springfield, Massachusetts as a player, Wooden was rehonored as a coach. He is the only man yet to be so recognized in both fields.

Wooden is the only man to be enshrined in the Basketball Hall of Fame as a player and a coach.

Cy Young

No one in major league baseball won more games than the 511 won by Denton True 'Cy' Young.

© National Baseball Hall of Fame & Museum

 DENTON TRUE "CY" YOUNG WAS A competitor *par excellence*. Not only did the 6-foot-2, 210-pound right-hander win more games (511) than any other pitcher in baseball history, it was the way in which he won those games.

Rube Waddell of the Philadelphia Athletics had shut down Young's Red Sox and pitcher Jesse Tannehill early in a 1904 five-game series, allowing a leadoff bunt single, then sending twenty-seven men down in order. Waddell and Young met later in the series and Waddell told him before the game, "I'm going to give you the same thing I gave Tannehill the other day." Young, a thirty-seven-year-old veteran who had seen pitchers come and go over the years, didn't think much of this brash third-year hurler. "I knew who he was, all right," he said. "I'd been watching him. He was a damned fine pitcher, but he ran his mouth quite

124

a bit. I figured he was calling me out and I had better do something about it." Though Waddell pitched another fine game, Young was better than that. He was perfect, as in no hits, no walks. Young made an eloquent statement on the mound, allowing only six balls out of the infield.

Young also pitched two no-hitters during his glorious twenty-two-year career and made winning a personal trademark. He won twenty or more games sixteen times. Some of his single-season records were unworldly. In 1892, his thirty-six victories came in forty-nine starts. His thirty-five-win season in 1895 represented more than half of the Cleveland Indians victories and was balanced by only ten losses. In this era of relief specialists, Young's outrageous numbers might not have been possible. There is a very good chance that no man will ever approach his victory total. Still, there is no evidence to suggest that he wouldn't have been among the game's very best pitchers even today.

Young was born on March 29, 1867, in Gilmore, Ohio. His enormous size made him an intimidating force on the mound, even in his youth. At the age of twenty-three, Young arrived in Cleveland of the National League and delivered a modest 9-7 record. He was a workhorse, as indicated by his 27-20 record and 423 innings pitched in 1891. Young won twenty games or more for the next fourteen consecutive years. In that span his 395 victories surpassed the career of every pitcher except Walter Johnson. Young's average season record over that time was a staggering 28-15.

By his third season, Young had seen all the hitters before and honed his pitches to an extraordinary level. He won thirty-six games, lost only eleven, fashioned a league-leading 1.93 earned-run average, and pitched nine shutouts. By 1903, when baseball was organized into its present form, Young was already

thirty-six years old. Yet he put together a 28-10 season and won two of the three games he pitched in the very first World Series. A 26-16 record followed and in 1908, at the age of forty-one, Young won twenty-one of thirty-three games. Young pitched for four teams during his career and accomplished another feat that may never be equaled: He is the only pitcher to ever win 200 games in both the National and American League.

In 1956, a year after Young's death, Ford Frick, the commissioner of baseball, had an idea. The Most Valuable Player awards in recent years had been going largely to everyday players like Joe DiMaggio and Yogi Berra. Frick concluded that a new award should be created to recognize pitchers only. Ever since, the outstanding pitcher in both the American and National League is honored with the Cy Young Award, a fitting tribute to the finest pitcher to ever grace a mound.

For fourteen consecutive seasons, Cy Young won twenty games or more; his career batting average was a rather robust .210.

Index